Foreword

This project of love has taken me several years to complete. I have travelled all over the world, virtually, seeking information so that I am able to present as accurate a story as possible about the life and times of my mother, Katherine Vera Kentish, who was known by everyone as Vera.

I have gleaned details from family information, her sister Florrie's book, from her own diaries, from my sisters Gwen, Marjory, Lorna and my brother Neil.

On a visit to Katanning we received so much help from the ladies at the library and the museum. They gave us a lot of information about the district, the family and directed us to Trove.

Trove, the digitised newspapers of Australia have been a real benefit with so much information being available to everyone. The digitised newspapers of the United Kingdom afforded me some insight to her family back in England.

Her ancestors lived for many years in France and there has been some conjecture about the name which was used during those times. I have elected to use the family name which pops up frequently during my research.

The reader will understand the extremely trying and difficult times in which she lived as a child and teenager. Then through the tough times of the depression and onto the difficult times during the Second World War. Provisions were very scarce during these times and many sacrifices were made.

Her Christian beliefs helped her through those times and she prospered.

My mum was such a gentle Christian lady and willing to do so much for her loved ones. She enjoyed the time that she could spend with her sisters and brothers and wished that those times could have been more frequent. Her work in the Church, mostly as a Sunday School teacher was respected by her students who gained an insight to the teachings of the Bible. She learnt so much from Pop Gomm and spent almost a lifetime passing this on to so many others.

My father was a dominant figure in the family but despite any difficulties that we could see as her children, she always rose above any situation and dealt with any problems head on with a loving and Christian attitude.

This book is dedicated to her and her life.

We miss you mum,

David Kentish

Contents

Chapter 1.

Hello, my name is Katherine Vera Kentish and this is my story.

I was born into this world on August 27, 1912 as Katherine Vera Lavis. By the time I was born my parents, Walter and Alice Lavis had ready for me, two sisters and two brothers. The older of them were born back in England before they emigrated to Australia but the younger of them, my brother Don was born on the ship on which they were travelling. But more of that later when it better fits into my story.

I know that this is the correct date of my birth, for my elder sister Florrie, who was nearly seven years old at the time of that great event of mine, used to tell me frequently that it was early morning when I arrived into this world. Mother was at home and was attended by one of our neighbour's wives, Mrs. Beeck, (*this name is pronounced "Beck"*) who had attended a good number of other local women in similar situations. Apparently I was named after her daughter, Vera but the Katherine came from an ancestral relative. There were no district nurses in those days and everyone had to help each other. The doctor was sent for but I was too eager to leave my confinement and experience the new life that was before me. My eldest sister, Dorothy, who was just eight and a half at the time, had to run to the nearby farm so they could saddle a horse and send a rider for the doctor but it seems that her run had been left a bit late or I was too eager to arrive. Either way, here I am and I'm going to stay for a very long time.

I really don't remember much of my early few years except that a couple of years before I was able to attend the local school, we had a large dark coloured snake slithering on the dirt floor of our bedroom and the younger ones, Molly & Myrtle (the twins), Chrissie and myself, were terrified and became more frightened as our Mother found and killed the snake with a green sapling. She then carried the awful thing outside and disposed of it in the chook pen. I think the chooks liked the fresh meat. The snake must have entered our bedroom through a very small hole in the wall of our home. Our house, like so many in the district at that time, was not very grand but it was our home.

The house was built before we settled in the district and was known as a "wattle and daub" construction. I had no idea what this meant for many years but I'll tell you now as it has some significance in the telling of my story. On the property on which the house was built, were a lot of naturally growing acacia trees which are locally called "wattle". The smaller trees have long thin stems. These stems were cut and tied into bundles. The bundles are then loaded into on old horse drawn dray and after being driven to the building site, unloaded and placed around the perimeter of the house. Several miles from the house there is a small creek which sometimes has water in it, usually in the winter time or after a thunderstorm in the summer. In the bottom of the damp creek there is usually mud and this was collected and also transported to the site. The mud was mixed with some straw which had been cut short and formed into a mixture just about like the dough that we used when we made bread. The wattle sticks were stuck in the ground and stood up to make the basis for the walls. These sticks are spaced at about two finger widths. The mud and straw mixture or "daub" was plastered by hand onto the sticks that are standing to complete the wall. Each day they could only work up about 2 feet or the daub would fall out if they went any higher. This process was continued until a height of about seven feet was reached. Then some larger sticks of timber were laid across the top of the walls to support a roof. I am told that in the early days this roof was made of brush which was cut from the surrounding land but my first memory of the roof was a corrugated iron roof from which we used to collect the rain water. Anyway that's enough about building our house, except to say that sometimes the daub would fall out leaving the occasional hole near ground level. The snake must have come into the bedroom through one of these small holes.

Another thing that I remember very well is that we did not have any floor coverings, just a hard packed earth floor. Apparently this was pretty much the norm for those days. When the settlers became more affluent, different flooring types were used but we'll get to that a bit later on when it fits into my story. Mother kept a very tidy house and my older siblings were always there to help too.

Father was always busy with his farm work. He spent quite a lot of time on our own farm but quite often he was away helping other farmers too. I realised later that he needed to do this to earn money to provide for our growing family. He was usually home the night before so we could all get cleaned up and ready to go to church on Sundays.

Church was always a very cheery time for us as that was when we spent some time with other people in the district that were so much like us. It also gave us the opportunity to dress up in our finest dresses and spend extra care doing our hair, scrub our nails, polish our shoes and so on. Father would drive us in his old buggy where he and Mother would sit on the seats at the front and the rest of us would sit in the tray at the back of the buggy. The track was rough in places and if Father drove his horse too fast we would bounce off the floor. That was always a thrill for us too but I don't think Father like us screaming with delight too much.

The years before I became of the age where I could attend school, provided me with the opportunity to do so many things. I would help Mother in the house of course, helping her cook, clean the house, look after

Chrissie (who was just one year younger than me) the twins (four years younger than me) and chase the chooks and ducks when they would not go into their yard at night. My eldest sister Dorothy made me a doll which I simply treasured. I know that Mother and Father didn't have any money to spend on such things so this was very special to me. She rolled up some cloth and with string, tied the cloth so that it represented legs, body, arms and head. Then she stitched in some horse's hair for the dolls hair and painted a face on the front of the head. I would play with my dolly whenever I had the chance but with a busy household like ours that was not very often. With my sisters only just a little younger than me, I do know that my dolly was shared around a lot and sometimes we would argue over whose turn it was to play with it. With scraps of cloth which Mother had left over from making our clothes, we would make different dresses for dolly and each of us had our own dresses which we made and when it was our turn to play with dolly we would dress it in the clothes that each of us has made. I stitched up a dress made from a scrap from Mothers pink check dress and that was my favorite one.

When I was about three years of age, I have a memory of us shifting house. We only moved about five miles onto another property which Father had purchased. Later years would reveal that he bought it from the Agricultural bank which had some severe stipulations.

He had to make it pay or lose his investment. Next year we moved back to our old home on the farm which was known as "Lyndhurst", so I assume that he wasn't successful. Anyway, it wasn't a very nice house. The walls were made from logs and the wind used to blow in between the gaps in the logs and Father didn't have time to make it right. Mother tried so many things to make it into a nice home but it was just too difficult. Dorothy, Ray and Florrie would chastise Father for forcing Mother to live in "such a dump" and soon we shifted back to our old home at "Lyndhurst". At about this time Father began working in the local grocers, Richardson's, in Woodanilling. I don't think he liked that job very much because he wasn't there for very long. He would prefer to be farming.

Our time at "Lyndhurst" was cut short and soon we were moving again to a place called Corrolup, which was about five miles southwest of Marracoonda. The older children still attended Marracoonda School but Mother was most upset that we should be housed near a man who showed no respect for her or her children. I don't understand the circumstances about this situation but it did cause a lot of disruption to our normally pleasant household.

So we moved again. Apparently Father had worked for Mr. Prosser before I came along and we moved to his farm and back to his little cottage he had for his workers. It was not long after this move that Mother

was about to have another baby. Shortly she was not
very well. Quite soon after the shift Mother presented us
with another sister. She was named Connie. Mother had
been taken to the hospital in Katanning a week or so
beforehand and it was left up to us children to keep the
house going. Father was off to work early in the
mornings for Mr. Prosser. Sometimes he was home at
lunch time but mostly we wouldn't see him till he
returned after dark from a day of hard work.
During this time we attended the church at
Marracoonda which was about half a mile from the
house. The older ones walked to the school in
Marracoonda again. While we were at Corrolup they
used to take the horse and buggy and spend nearly an
hour each way. Dorothy, Ray, Florrie and now Don
were going off to school at Marracoonda each week
morning, so just Mother, me and the younger girls were
left at home to keep the home running. Mother needed
to rest often as she didn't seem to be too well. So
Chrissie and I kept watch over the twins and baby
Connie while Mother rested. I remember kneeling
beside my bed each night before climbing in and saying
my prayers. I still remember the words. "God bless
Mother and Father and my sisters and brothers and all
of our friends and dolly, Amen.
We treasured these times with Mother and she taught us
a lot about dressmaking as she was an assistant to a
draper in England before she met Father. She told us of

so many things that I forget them but sometimes these memories do return. She showed us how to stitch the cloth so it would not fray at the edges without wasting material. In later years this would come in very handy as we would need to make our own clothes.

We tried to grow a garden but the lack of water in the summer times made this impossible to keep the garden growing all year round. But in spite of the many difficulties we did grow some of our own vegetables and Mother even had a small flower garden by the front of the house. At the end of summer or more correctly into autumn we had a show of Easter lilies by the front door. I remember Mother was very proud of these beautiful flowers. A couple of fig trees did survive and I remember picking a few figs that the parrots didn't get to first. One of the trees produced figs of a pale colour while the other had a dark flesh and tasted better. I was always the one to climb to the top of the fig trees and pick the figs that everyone else couldn't reach from the ground.

I remember my first day at school, it was summer time in the new year of 1918. Dorothy, Ray, Florrie, Don and I walked the mile from Prosser's Cottage to the Marracoonda School. The lady teacher was Miss Keast and she seemed only just a few years older than my big sister, Dorothy. The girls helped me sort out the things that I needed for my first day and I had on my prettiest dress that Dorothy, Mother and I had made. I was wearing Florrie's old shoes which I had shined up. We walked along the road and to the top of the hill where the school was. Some time ago a few of the other children had planted some trees around the school yard and these have just started to grow. The sheep and cattle that grazed in the paddock alongside the school yard always took my fancy and I spent some time patting them and talking to them through the fence in between classes.

Although my sisters had shown me how to draw and write and read, school was a new experience for me. Sitting at that funny desk that moved each time I shifted on the seat. Pencils would roll off the desk onto the floor. I had to pick them up many times before I mastered the art of sitting still. It was very difficult for me to do that, as I had been so active around the house helping Mother.

So a new period in my life began. From Monday to Friday we had to do the chores around the house to help Mother, eat our breakfast and then it's off to school after we had packed our lunches. Sometimes we had to run as we always seemed to run out of time and I didn't want to miss any lessons. Then after school it was time to run home again and do more chores to help Mother about the house. I always had to collect the eggs from the chooks who had their yard out behind the house. If I left them overnight some would break or the crows would fly in and rob the nest if the old chook wasn't sitting on the eggs. When I collected the eggs in the winter mornings I would hold them in my hands as they were nice and warm but I couldn't carry them all like that so after a few minutes they went into the basket so I could carry them back to the kitchen.

Saturdays saw us helping with the washing and this was hard work. The boys would collect the water from the old well and bring the buckets full of water into the wash-house. Mother had acquired a cement wash trough which had two segments and this was great for washing and rinsing. With that awful smelling yellow soap I would rub the clothes up and down the washboard then rinse them out before they could be pegged onto the wire that Father had put up for us to dry the clothes. It sagged in the middle so Ray cut a sapling with a "Y" at the top to hold the wire higher so the clothes wouldn't drag in the dirt. It was not a lot of fun but we all needed clean clothes and everyone else had their own jobs to do. Dorothy did sometimes help me with the washing of the clothes but Florrie always seemed to have been busy somewhere doing something else. I couldn't reach the clothes line so when it was time to hang them out I had to get Dorothy or Florrie to do that part of the job for me. We had a big galvanized iron tub that the clothes would go into after they were rinsed and it was always too heavy for me to lift. That's when one the others would have to help me too. But as I grew older and bigger I was able to do this by myself.

Sunday was the day when we attended church or
Sunday school. While the parents in the district
attended the church service, all of us children would be
taught Sunday school in the room out the back of the
church. I was fascinated by the stories of Jesus Christ
and the work that he did with the children. At home we
always say grace before we had our meals and read the
Bible after breakfast. Mother would read from it when
Father was away or had to start work before we had our
breakfast, so the stories of the Bible were not new to me
but having someone else tell the story made such a
difference, that I felt like I was learning so much more.
About the first time that I remember the town of
Katanning was when we took a ride in the buggy when
the armistice was signed to signify the end of the Great
War. The older ones and I had a great time because that
day was a Monday holiday and we didn't have to go to
school. We all bundled into the buggy and as usual we
older children sat on the floor of the buggy whilst
Mother and Father sat in the front at so Father could
drive the buggy and Mother nursed Connie on her lap. I
think the twins may have been seated between them but
I'm not sure about that. But it was a great day out and
being able to do something different even for just a day
put big smiles on everyone's face. Of course I didn't
understand what it was all about but in later years I did
learn that many of Mother and Father's relatives were
living in England and they were grateful that the war

had come to an end. I do know that we lost several relatives during that conflict.

Father didn't seem to be happy working for Mr. Prosser. He liked it better when he was working on his own land and soon his itchy feet took us to moving again. This time we moved right away from the Marracoonda-Woodanilling area and to a place to the north-east of Katanning that was called the "Mean Mahn" district. It has a name change over the years and today it's known as the "Coblinine" district. This property which was called "Twynesdale" was about twelve miles along Warren Road. The shift of about twenty miles took us nearly a week to complete. Florrie and I took turns to lead the old milking cow along the track to the new place and one of the boys would ride out to us and stay with us in the bush for the night. We sat around the fire and sang songs or then Ray would tell us a story as we sat under the stars. There were many stars all shining brightly in the night sky. They made such a pretty picture.

The house which Father had selected for us was not very nice and was very hard to clean because of the dirt floor and no ceiling. But the land was supposed to be fairly good according to Mr. Prosser. Father said he would build a new house just as soon as the next crop was harvested but it just didn't seem to be a priority to him. But Mother persisted with the dusty, dirty conditions and did her best to keep us all clean, fed, clothed and safe.

Father had a few sheds to keep his equipment in but they needed repair too and he was kept ever so busy. He was out before breakfast mending this and fixing that, then back into the house for breakfast. Then he was out there again until he joined Mother for lunch. Then he was off again doing his mending of machinery, fences and sheds until dark. He would wash up and change into clean clothes and join us for the evening meal. When he had all of these jobs done he would go off and do some work for some of the other farmers around our home to help them too. His outside work obviously brought in some badly needed cash to help support the family but this didn't become evident to me until I became older.

A small orchard behind the house had many trees which had been established by the previous owner but they didn't produce much in the way of fruit. Dorothy said that they needed some special attention but with Father being so busy it was left to Mother to organise or do the work and she was just not up to the task.

Ray, Dorothy, Florrie, Don, Chrissie and I attended the local school at Mean Mahn. It was a quarter mile off the Warren Road just down Newton Road and was about 5 miles from our home. My goodness, that was such a long way for us children to travel to and from school. Each morning one of the boys, usually Ray, would catch the horse and prepare the harness and hitch up the buggy. We had to leave very early each day and arrive home late again as it seemed to take such a long time to complete the journey. Each way was about an hour and the road was very rough so we had our share of shakes and jerks by the time we got to school or home, depending on which way we were going. Some days when father needed the buggy, we would all ride on the horse's bare back. It was a bit of a squeeze but it beats walking.

Luckily there was a hitching rail for the horses at school and most days would see six or more horses tethered there munching on some hay or straw. I remember that our teacher was a Miss Gladys Stade, who was not long out of teacher school. Many of the other children used to disrespect her as she was so young and took a while to develop her teaching abilities. This did disrupt our classes and I remember that at least on one occasion Florrie would stand up in class and speak her mind to them. It did seem to quieten down a bit. This school was not as nice as the one that was at Marracoonda.

I found out much later that this school building had been shifted from another site to here just a few years before we moved to Mean Mahn. Apparently it had to be shifted because there was not many children left near the place where it was near the corner of Warren and Withers roads. Today there is a plaque on a stone to show where the original site was and another to show the place where it was when I attended school.

Mother was carrying her eleventh child and we were all excited in wondering whether we were going to have a little brother or another sister. I was told much later that Mother's fourth child, a boy named Stanley had died a short time after birth. Mother was always very tired and that meant that she needed to rest a lot and we children were required to do more around the house. She had her favorite deck chair and she would sit in this for quite a while, simply resting. It was very difficult leaving her each school day to look after the younger ones while we were away at school. The twins were just four years old with Connie being just two. I don't remember how she cared for them while we were at school but I don't remember any great disasters that needed to be fixed up when we got home again. Just into the New Year, Mother was confined into the hospital at Katanning. The older girls did a splendid job of caring for all of us while Mother was away. Father would visit Mother when he could and sometimes he would stay overnight in town just to be with her as much as was possible. On the nineteenth of January 1920, Mother delivered to the world another of her daughters. She would be named Margaret Patricia and she turned out to be the last to be born to our family. I was about seven and a half years old at the time and it was all very exciting for us. It would be such fun to help look after a new baby. Of course I helped look after the others but now that I had grown up some, it would be so much better.

Now that Father had ten mouths to feed he began working almost feverishly to provide for us. He always seemed to be coming or going and not spending much time with us as a family except for Sundays, when he did spend more time if his work allowed but these times seemed very short.

Mother was still very tired much of the time and continued to spend a lot of her time resting. The old deck chair was moved around the house so she could be out of the wind and just in the sun on cooler days. About this time, 1921, my eldest brother, Ray, left school as he needed to work with Father to help raise money for the family. Apparently Father's crops where not always successful and he needed the extra help for the work he had contracted for with some other local farmers. They would stay away all week and get home on the weekends. Their work was heavy and due to the clearing and burning that they were doing, their clothes were always very dirty and took such a time to wash and dry them.

Dorothy left home too and she took on a job as house keeper but soon began training as a teacher. She held many teaching positions around the district and remained there for many years. Dorothy loved horses and she often participated in local shows. She did very well at the 1918 Katanning Agricultural Show and the next week at the Tambellup Agricultural Show in the "pair of hacks, ladies driving competition". She had the reputation in the district as being a very accomplished horse woman.

Dorothy was away from home most of the time now as she had gainful employment with various families as governess. Her wages were sent back home to supplement the family income. Of course I didn't understand all this talk about money at the time but as I became older I learned to recognise the signs that I didn't know of at that early age. Both Dorothy and Florrie have told me so much over the years to fill in the blanks for me from my childhood days.

The end of school in 1921 was memorable for me as it was the last year that either of my older sisters would be at school. Dorothy had left last year and at the end of this year Florrie was to leave and take a job at the hospital in Katanning, so she too could send her wages home for the family. But before she left we all got together and made a presentation at the break-up at the Mean Mahn School where we attended. All of the students did some little thing like singing or reciting or putting on a play. The older ones did a play of "Cinderella", even the teacher, Miss Stade, took part too! I remember standing up in front of everyone shaking like a leaf and doing a recitation. But I can't for the life of me remember what the poem was about.

Perhaps because I was so nervous that I have forgotten but that was such a long time ago.

In September of 1922, Mother had several visits to the doctor. Father said that the doctor and he were concerned that Mother should be so unwell for such a long time after little Margaret arrived. I had not long ago turned ten years old and I was beginning to understand a lot more about Mother's health. She was not able to do much around the house for the family and found it difficult to attend church. But she always put on a brave face and never complained but even I could see in her face that she was very unwell.

In February 1923 in the middle of a heatwave, Mother was admitted to the hospital in Katanning once again. This time the reason for her visit there was not to bring home another baby. Mother had shown no signs of getting better. Father was very concerned and after several visits to the doctor she was kept in hospital. The heat may have caused her health problem or made it worse but the doctor wanted her near where he could look after her. Father told us that the doctor thought that she might return home soon but time seemed to drag on so.

However she did return home!

Florrie returned home from her work and soon after that Dorothy too returned home to care for Mother. Later Florrie told me that she slept next to Mother on another deck chair just to keep her company during the hot summer nights. They were outside as the house was so hot inside even at night.

Connie and the twins were cared for by some neighbours and I stayed at home to care for Margaret until school began in February. Then I saw Connie and the twins when they arrived at school with the families who they were staying with. We spent all of our time at school together just to spend time as we felt very close to each other. The other girls were not very happy with the families that they were staying with as they were being bullied by the boys.

March the first 1923 was a very dark day for me as my Mother passed away while we were at school and we didn't get to know of this until we returned home in the afternoon. It seemed that having eleven babies, working so hard, putting up with such poor conditions added to the fact that our food was not always the most nutritious caused her to become so ill. Everyone was devastated and the household was very dark for many days. We all huddled together and cried for a long time. The next few days just seemed a blur. Things got done, we were fed but I don't know how.

I remember the funeral being held at the church. So many people attended, a lot of people from the local Mean Mahn area and also many from the Woodanilling and Marracoonda areas too. So many people to pay their respects to my Mother. After the service we travelled to the cemetery just out of Katanning where our Mother was laid to rest. She had been so busy in her lifetime and put up with such poor conditions to live in, that a rest is exactly what was needed and to be taken into God's care in heaven.

Father was struck particularly badly and didn't even do any work for several weeks and there were the small children to care for too!

Dorothy would stay for a few days but had to return to her job. I think her income was so important to the survival of the family.

After some time away from our home Florrie returned home just before Dorothy had left. She was going to look after the house and us children.

The boys and I helped with the running the house and milking the cows and the younger ones did what they could to help but Margaret was just three years old and needed our care. Connie at five years old had to look after Margaret most of the time and sometimes the twins would step up too.

I do remember still collecting the eggs though. The walk to the chook yard was hard with so many tears in my eyes but I got there and back alright. I remember sitting down with the chooks and talking to them about my Mother and all of the great things she had done for me. I even took my old dolly down with me as it seemed to comfort me a just a little. I'd take some of the wheat from the chook feeder and have them take it from my hand as I held them in my lap just talking quietly to them all the time. Spending so much time by myself probably was not the best thing for me but at the time it was what I thought that I needed to do.

At night we spent some time sitting around the table after having the meal prepared by Florrie, talking and after a few nights Father began talking about the past and how he may have done things differently. He told us some of his family history as he understood it and what he could remember of what Mother had told him of her family. It made a great story to all of us but it wasn't until years later that I fully understood the meaning of what he had told us.

The very dark days after Mother passed away became less dark as the days wore on.

Chapter 2.

Slowly our lives returned to some sort of normality with Florrie being the main person in charge of the house, doing most of the cooking, which had improved a lot since her first efforts, and making some dresses for us girls as we grew out of the old ones. Of course we have hand-me-downs but always the older ones need something to step into. She tried to do what Mother used to do, some time ago.

But she wasn't Mother!

Father's financial problems came to a head. Florrie told us that the bank manager had been to visit and Father was very upset with the outcome of the meeting. It seems that the bank could no longer support our Father's outstanding debts and that he would need to forgo the farm that he owed money on, to the bank. He had to clear his debts in the bankruptcy court in 1923 and then he began a new start to life.

He had previously bought some land not far away from where we lived and he and the boys and Florrie set about building a new house.

On this farm a dam had been build some years before by the previous owner and they used to cart water from this dam, straw from the paddock and clay from around the dam to make brick batts. Each one weighed about fifty pounds (22 kilos) and were stacked onto a trolley that was drawn by the horses and carted to where the house was to be built. A neighbour who was a builder before the war helped them with ideas and plans. After the foundations were laid, the laying of the bricks took place very slowly. It took many weeks of them working hard to have our house completed. My younger sisters and I would try to help too. We would help mix up some of the clay to make the bricks and then make some of the mud that was used to go between the bricks to hold them together. After we had mixed it up of course, Ray or Don or Father would add some white powder, lime I think, to the mix and we weren't allowed to play with that mixture.

Sometimes some of the mud would find its way onto our faces and we had lots of fun playing with the mud and getting dirty. Luckily the boys would bring up some more water from the dam and we could wash ourselves and our clothes before Florrie got too upset. Oh, how she scolded us for getting ourselves and our clothes into such a mess.

We tried to keep out of their way as they were working but we were having some fun. Sometimes Don or Ray would yell at us to get out of the way. We always took notice and of course moved out of the way but our attention was more on having a bit of fun than doing as they told us. There wasn't much that we could do that was fun, anyway.

Eventually the four rooms with a verandah was completed with a wash-house out the back. The new long-drop toilet, or dunny as Don called it, was out just past the wash-house.

The small kitchen was on the back verandah and it was very basic. It had the stove from the old house and a bench on which the washing-up bowl could stand. The old table was a bit wobbly but it was all we had. All of our old stuff that was in the old house was moved over to the new house and after several weeks of working together before and after school we soon had made it into our home. It was not very grand and the walls were rough and dusty inside but we did have a floor. The windows were glass so now we could see out and let in some light without all of the drafts that we were used to. The chimney of the kitchen began to sizzle the first time the fire was lit but it soon settled down and Florrie was now cooking some nice meals again.

Things seemed to settle down with Florrie taking the part of the house Mother. She had learnt some new techniques on how to make our clothes and now they did look a lot better. Father helped with some suggestions too as he was in the clothing business back in England. They were not the latest fashion but we did have the opportunity to have some new material sent out to us so she could do her dressmaking. Florrie also mastered the art of making bread. Her first couple of loaves were a bit tough but I don't remember too much being thrown out.

Dorothy was the head teacher at the school at Wilgoyne, so we didn't get to see her as often as we would have liked. But the Sunday Times newspaper did print an article that we all enjoyed reading about the official opening of the school where she received glowing reports.

Florrie must have liked being busy because not only was she looking after the house and us children she spent some time working with a group of locals to raise money to build a hall at Merribin, half way between home and the school. After the money was raised the locals banded together and soon the hall was completed along with a timber floor. After a piano was acquired, dances were held there about each month. Now we had something else to dress up for. But the lack of cash always kept us thrifty and looking at ways to alter our existing dresses to make them more up to date and too our liking. The new hall was busy with parties and functions most weekends. It was at one of the functions that Florrie met a young man or beau. His name was Harrold Edwards and soon they held their wedding in the hall in August, 1927. She left us behind as she went off to live with Harold about 15 miles up the road at Bullock Hills. We did keep in touch but only saw her occasionally after that. She would visit on her way from there to Katanning or on the way back to their farm but frequently the younger girls were at school and missed seeing her unless she stayed over-night. I did so miss her being around.

At fourteen, I now had the charge of the house, looking after the younger girls and Father. Making the meals for them and keeping the house in good order with washing the clothes and looking after the little ones too. The boys were out working on other farms, so at least I didn't have to cook for them but the house was certainly much quieter with them away. By jingies, I do miss them though.

Chrissie was about thirteen and was a big help but everyone just got stuck into whatever jobs needed to be done. Florrie would drop in from time to time just to help out and guide me in the right direction.

Dorothy who had a teaching position away from Katanning had met a young man named Abel Austin. He was a returned soldier from the front in France and worked with the young people in Katanning, teaching them Ju-Jitsu. He had learned this in the armed forces and thought the discipline would benefit so many of the young people around the districts. I tried it once or twice but could not get my coordination right to perfect some of the moves. They met each other frequently and in early March 1928 began the arrangements for their wedding. Dorothy and I had always got along well. I think we understood each other in a way that just didn't seem to work with Florrie, who always seemed just a bit too bossy. Dorothy asked me to be her bridesmaid and

Connie to be her flower-girl. Well, we were over the moon with excitement and agreed immediately. Now we had to start work on our gowns as this was such a special occasion. The materials were purchased by Dorothy from Mr. Bateman the draper in Austral Terrace in town and we found some patterns that suited us and we set about making the gowns between doing all of the other jobs that needed to be done around the house. The design was just like the one that Mother had described to Dorothy which she had worn at her wedding, when she married Father.

My dress had a drop waist with a cord around the waist. It had a round neck with long sleeves and it was bell shaped at the bottom. It was three quarter length with lace sewn into the bottom hem. The cotton fabric for the dress was soft to the touch so that it felt almost like silk. I remember wearing white silk stockings with dress shoes which had a strap below the ankle. I had my hair shoulder length with a band on the forehead. My bouquet was assembled from mixed flowers. Some of these came from the garden at home with a selection of wild flowers which grew beside the road.

We carefully followed the pattern and after a lot of measuring and double checking, we cut out the pattern from the material. Although we were very excited we had to be careful that we didn't make a mistake as we could not afford to buy any more material. Each of the hems and joins were very carefully stitched by hand just the way Mother had taught us. Dorothy even stayed with us for a few days while we did most of the cutting and tacking just to be satisfied that we had it just right. After she had left, we went about carefully hand stitching all of the components together. I think we did a jolly good job of the dresses with each of us stitching our own garment. Stitching the lace around the bottom hem was a bit of a bother as it was so fine but it turned out remarkably well and we were very pleased with the result of our handiwork. What a pity Mother wasn't here to see what we had achieved. She would have been so proud of our work. Well it did bring tears to my eyes again as I remembered Mother and I could just imagine her sitting there closely inspecting my work and giving me her special little praise that she always gave us when we did a good job.

The excitement was building for Connie and me but especially for dear Dorothy who was to be married in just a couple of days. We were having trouble containing our excitement as the special day approached. We didn't have much to look forward to in those days and this was going to be something super special.

The day finally arrived and after we had completed our early morning chores, Father drove us into Katanning in the horse and buggy. The wedding was for late morning so we had time once we got there to change into our brand new handmade dresses. We had a tall mirror to dress by and I was very proud of my handiwork and Connie looked amazing too. Then in came Dorothy and she was just so pleased that all of our careful work looked so grand, just for her special day.

The ceremony seemed to take just a couple of minutes but I know it took about an hour. The special hymns were sung and then the minister pronounced them man and wife and they moved off to the registry to complete the paperwork which has my signature on it as a witness to the special event. The wedding breakfast was excellent with much of the work being done beforehand by Dorothy and her friends from the district and the school where she was teaching.

We were extremely tired when Father finally turned the last corner into our gateway that opened onto the track which took us home. Such a wonderful day that will remain in my memory for ever. I think that was the best night's sleep I have had 'till that time. We carefully packed away our frocks to keep them for another special occasion later. We didn't know what it was yet. Maybe? Although this arrangement worked well for about a year, Father wasn't happy. Maybe the family needed the money as he suggested that I get a job working with another family and send the money back home to help keep the house. I was very upset with this arrangement but Father did manage to get me a job as home help for a family out near Nyabing.

That was such a long way from home and Chrissie had to take her turn at looking after everything now. We had worked well together after Dorothy had moved on so I think she is capable of doing the job well.

Father took me into Katanning in the horse and buggy and I went out next morning with Mr. Withers who had the mail contract. He collected the mail from the train at Katanning and delivered it to the outlying towns with his two horse team and buggy. The Kruger's[1] farm was just a mile from the main road so he dropped me off there and I walked the rest of the way carrying my old bag that contained some of my clothes. Father had arranged this position for me and thought that these were nice Christian people. It took me several days to get to understand them as they didn't speak very good English. I had to be up an hour before the sun so I could get the fire going so I could cook breakfast for the family. Mrs. Kruger seemed lazy and left me to do all of the housework and cooking. She was always yelling at me because she thought that I wasn't doing the job to her satisfaction. I burst into tears sometimes but I made sure that she didn't see me crying. After their evening meal was completed, I could have mine after they had left the kitchen. Then I had to wash the dishes and clean up after them before I could get to my bed for a rest. That was many hours after dark. So I didn't get more

---

[1] I have changed the name here so that I don't offend anyone.

than a few hours' sleep before I had to get up and repeat the same things the next day.

Oh how I hated that place.

I never thought that I would hate anyone but I think I came very close with that family. The two boys were nasty to me but their daughter, who was the youngest was nice to me and helped when her Mother couldn't see. In the second week, Mr. Kruger began yelling at me just before breakfast and Mrs. Kruger took on the same ranting when he left the house. That was when I burst into tears in front of her and told that I would finish immediately and go back to my family. She must have realised what a state I was in and tried to be nice and asked me to stay but my mind was made up and nothing would make me change it, especially for them. After packing what clothes I had in my bag I walked back to the main road and began the track back to Katanning. I was fortunate that Mr. Withers and the mail buggy was on the road at that time and he took me back into Katanning where I stayed the night. Next morning, which was a Saturday, I began the ten mile walk back to my family's home at Twynesdale farm. The bag with my clothes became too heavy for me so when I went past the school I hid it amongst the bushes beside the road. I'd get the twins to pick it up on Monday, on their way back from school in the horse and buggy.

Father was very surprised to see me at home when he walked in after he had finished his work. After explaining what had happened and how I was treated he told me that he was happy to have me at home again. I soon got back into the swing of things in our home again. It sure was great to be home among those who you love and love you!

Chrissie had left school at fourteen and now that I had come home she went to work for a nice family out towards Bullock Hills about five miles from Florrie and Harold. She seemed to like the work and I'm sure some of the money we needed to spend when we went shopping had come from her.

Father seemed to get itchy feet again and was looking at moving. He soon found some land just six miles to the south of Badgebup, which was about twenty miles to the east from Katanning, so it was a long way.

Father sold the land that he owned at Mean Mahn, which was called "Twynesdale" and once again we began the shift. This time it took us more than a week to drive the sheep, cows and horses the distance while we camped out under the stars for several nights until we reached the new property, which is known in the district as "Blair Athol". The old house which had been built ten or more years earlier was in fair condition and soon the younger girls and I had it whipped into some sort of shape to make it comfortable for us to live in. The boys did help too but Father needed them to work with him to mend the fences and the couple of old sheds that were already there. That was in the summer of 1927 when I was just over fifteen years old.

The little church at Badgebup, just like the church at Marracoonda, was built of stone and was a very pleasant place to attend the Sunday Church services. It would take us about an hour to drive the horse there with the girls and me in the buggy with Father. Sometimes the boys would ride their horses alongside the buggy too if they were home from their jobs on other farms. There was no ordained Christian minister in the district so the local men used to preach at the church as "lay preachers". Several of the men put a different slant on the teachings of the Bible but I always found it very interesting. One of the lay preachers who came out from Katanning to take the Sunday school and the church service was a tall slim man that we got to know as Mr. J.C. Gomm. He would turn up about half an hour before the services were due to start and he was usually accompanied by his wife, Mary. She was such a lovely person who had difficulty in walking any great distance. We got to know this couple very well and they would quite often visit our home after the services and even stay for the night as it's not such a good idea to travel with the horse and sulky in the dark. We did so enjoy their company around the dinner table. It made such a change from just Father and us girls for dinner.

The boys usually had gone back to the farms where they were working by this time of day.

Father was not very happy and frequently seeks company of other adults for conversation. He made the decision to get some help with the family and advertised in the local and state newspapers for a lady to keep house and look after the children. We didn't know about this of course until a lady turned up at our door asking for Mr. Walter D. Lavis. Apparently she had responded to the advert and Father had asked her to begin work as soon as she was able.

The cottage had three rooms in which we slept but they were not all bedrooms. We older ones, the twins Molly and Myrtle and me, did our best to be comfortable on the verandah while the little ones, Connie and Margaret, had a room inside. Chrissie was sent out when she turned 14 and was working for a family on their farm, out near Bullock Hills, about 25 miles to the east. We didn't see much of her now that we were at Blair Athol. Father had his own bedroom which he needed to share with the boys when they were at home for their short visits or sometimes they would sleep in the shed with the hay and the horse feed. So when this lady came to live with us, it put such a strain on all of us as we all had to share the verandah for sleeping. It was a squeeze but we all worked together and for the most part it was good. We even slept two to a bed now. This was good in

the winter we could all keep warm but in the summer
months the heat kept us from sleeping properly.

Mrs. Dunkley was a good cook once she learnt that we
didn't have much with which to prepare our meals. She
encouraged Father to prepare a vegetable garden so she
could prepare some better meals for us. He
begrudgingly cut his working days shorter so he could
do this for her. After a few months the food that she
grew in the gardens made a big improvement to our
meals. She bought some ducklings and some of these
eventually found their way onto our table after she
cooked them in the Dutch oven.

Most of the eggs and cream and butter that we
produced was sold in town when Father went in on
Fridays. I think he bartered with other farmers too for
more feed for the horses and cows and chooks.

Mrs. Gertrude Dunkley cared for the younger ones who
were now 11, 9 and 8 years old. She didn't seem to care
too much for me as I was the oldest one at home now
but I did help here with all of the work that was needed
to be done around the house and the yard.

Like always, we all had our little jobs to do. I had to
milk the two cows twice each day, make sure they had
enough feed and keep their water clean. When the milk
had settled I would skim off the cream and made butter
from what cream we didn't have at the table but that
wasn't much anyway. Connie had to keep the chooks
and ducks locked up at night and keep their water

clean. One night she got a bit side-tracked and the gate was left open. During that night in the middle of summer, there was a terrible racket coming from the chooks. Father knew immediately what the problem was and he raced out with his old shotgun. He shot and killed the fox but it had already killed four of the best laying hens. Mrs. Dunkley would remind Connie in no uncertain terms that she must never forget to shut the gate to the chook yard at night time when they all went in to roost.

She had been with our family for just under a year when Father and Mrs. Dunkley had an urgent trip to Perth on the train. They went in to town as usual on Friday and we found out later that they had left the horse and buggy with one of his friends. They caught the morning train and arrived in Perth that afternoon. They were back home again Tuesday afternoon and they had become married while they were in Perth. We didn't even know that they intended to marry so it was a complete surprise to us all. So now Father insisted that we call her Mother. Well, this did not go down very well at all with us children. We had all known and loved our Mother very much and it took us all a long time to get used to the idea of calling her Mother. About the only good thing that I remember coming from the marriage is that the younger girls could move back into the inside bedroom and give us all some more room for our beds on the verandah. They could even have a bed each so that made them a little happier.

Slowly, so very slowly our new mother began to change. Where she used to be as a caring person to each of us, she began picking at every little thing that we did wrong. Many of the things we had been doing for years now seemed to be wrong. We could not seem to do anything correct. She just seemed to change everything. She made us tell her when one of the others did something wrong, so that they could be scolded. We soon learned from this and we agreed that we wouldn't see anyone doing anything wrong so she would not accuse us. It made us all so unhappy but Father could not see what was happening.

I had words with Father about the way that we were being treated now but nothing that I could say would make him see what we could see happening.

I was always in trouble. I was even milking the cow the wrong way. The cream was being scooped off the top of the milk in the wrong fashion. The butter was rancid. The milk went off too quick. The mice got into the cupboard and ate the flour and cereals and it was all my fault. But none of these things was even happening, well, with the exception of the mouse problem which we all giggled about when she couldn't see us. She visited Florrie and Dorothy a couple of times and tried to set them against us too but they were aware of what was happening and would have none of her nonsense.

I was not at all happy at home.

On a Sunday we went to church and Sunday school where Mr. Gomm was taking the service that day. He was invited to our home after the service and he stayed the night. I think the younger girls let him use their bed and they crawled in with us older girls. Mrs. Gomm had not been well and was at home recovering from an operation which Doctor Campbell-Pope had carried out in the hospital at Katanning. After a discussion with Father it was decided that I would go and live with them in town and help around their house, keep Mrs. Gomm company and assist her in the recovery from her illness. They were such lovely gentle Christian folk and it certainly would be a pleasure living in their house with them.

Well, when Father told me this news, I was so surprised and excited that I asked how soon I could go. It was arranged that I would go with them the next morning. What I didn't know but did learn about later, was that Father had required Mr. Gomm to pay him the six shillings a week that I would earn to be paid directly to him. After me being with the Gomms for six months, this information was shared with me by Mr. Gomm. When next I saw Father I complained to him. We discussed the situation with Mr. Gomm and Father grudgingly agreed the let me have three shillings a week of my earnings. The rest was to go to help feed the family at home.

It didn't take me long to get my few things packed up ready to go. I only had a few dresses and some shabby working clothes. A pair of boots and a pair of shoes. They all fitted into an old sugar bag.

I was very sad to be leaving the twins, as well as Connie and Margaret. I would be happy to be away from my step-Mother but Father seems glad to see me go and I was very hurt and surprised about this.

Next morning we were ready to leave just after breakfast. It was very hard saying goodbye to the girls. We hugged and cuddled for a while then she stepped in and told us to behave and for me to get on the buggy. I gave Father a hug and kiss but I could not bring myself to kiss my step-Mother goodbye. I shook her hand instead enduring her cold glare. Father did not seem to be too pleased with my action. "That's not becoming of a Christian person to be so rude" he told me. I wondered if he saw her actions were as becoming of a Christian person in any way.

So now a new chapter in my life begins as we trundle down the road with Mr. Gomm in the buggy on the way to a new life living with them in their home.

I wondered how I would like it. I do know that I would miss the girls desperately but they may come to town from time to time to see us and I would attend with the Gomms when they visited the local churches. We could catch up then.

 I wonder!

Chapter 3

In June 1929 I accompanied Mr. Gomm in the buggy on the way to a new life living with them, away from my step-mother. I certainly would not miss her but I was very sad at not being able to see father and the girls as I had done whilst living at home. I am going to miss them so much.

We approached his home in Arbour Street, just opposite the Boy's Grammar School in Katanning from the laneway at the back of the house where, inside the gate, he had a small stable for his horse and a shed for his buggy. He had built them himself and they did look very grand. A small vegetable garden was flourishing behind the house which looked very neat and tidy from the back. The lavatory sits at the back fence. Mr. Gomm told me that the night cart comes weekly to empty the pan, so that's one job I needn't have to do, emptying the dunny pan.

 The wash-house was between the house and the vegie garden. In the wash-house were a pair of heavy cement troughs, like a big long trough but with a divider in the middle. It was just the right height so that it makes it easier to stand at while scrubbing the clothes with the washing board. Each section had its own drain and plug. Close by was the copper, which stood in the corner. It was a shining new looking copper but with a few dents. It was set into one of the cast iron stands.

There is a small stack of wood beside the copper. A wash board was hanging on a hook on the wall. On a shelf above the wash-trough were a few bars of hard soap, so I could see that it wasn't going to be too hard doing the washing here. The clothes line is supported by two poles with pivoting cross arms. There is about forty feet of line, so that should be plenty for this household. A hard packed gravel pathway leads up to the back verandah with several steps at the edge of the verandah. A handrail at the side of the steps makes it easier for Mrs. Gomm to negotiate them when she needs to visit the back yard.

Mr. Gomm carries my bags into the house and there's Mrs. Gomm to welcome me in open arms. It took me only a short time to feel completely at home. Her welcome was so lovely. She had recently been in hospital and is now recovering well from the operation which she had had done there.

Presently I was shown to my room which had two beds in it with a dressing table, wardrobe and a washstand under the window. Lovely curtains blocked the outside glare from entering the room which looked so cosy and warm. The window has glass in it so that'll keep out the rain and those nasty winter chilling drafts. They gave me ample time to unpack and then we sat down and discussed what I would be doing to help in their home. As Mrs. Gomm had difficulty in walking, I was to do the cooking, cleaning and the dishes. The house was to be swept each day and the dusting done once a week. I was to be on hand when Mrs. Gomm needed to walk around the house, just in case she need assistance. Her balance was not too good and her left leg drags a little when she walked, making it difficult for her to do most of the jobs that they had just outlined for me to do.

But the house was very tidy and clean and I could see that it would be a simple task to do the jobs that they had outlined. The smooth wooden floor was polished so that would be easy to sweep and mop. The walls were lined and painted so that should take care of those pesky spiders. The windows all had glass in them so the dust, rain and wind won't be a problem there either. The icebox was close to the back door so the iceman didn't have to traipse through the whole house just to refill it. I didn't know what it was at first as we didn't have one at home on the farm and the milk would go off after a day or so, the butter would become rancid after a few days, particularly in the summer time. The old Coolgardie Safe which we had, kept things just a little cooler than the outside temperature but it did need to be kept wet and this sometimes didn't get done on time. So this was another thing that was new to me.

The wood-box for the kitchen stove was filled from the outside but the wood was very close by the stove. The sitting room was at the front of the house and had three lovely comfortable chairs set out in front of the fireplace. Another wood-box that filled from the outside was beside the fireplace so everything was just so convenient. The main bedroom was at the front of the house and separated from the sitting room by a passage which had the front door at the far end. It had a lovely section of leadlight in the centre of the front door that depicted Jesus with his crook and a lamb by his feet. On the front porch is a pretty sign that tells me that the home is called "Holmleigh". It was named after the house where Mrs. Gomm had lived from childhood in England. The third bedroom was just behind the main bedroom and it too had two beds in it.

Mrs. Gomm was so pleased that I liked her home and she explained that Mr. Gomm had built it himself, soon after they had come to live in Katanning. He has been working in the building and construction industry for many years and was currently working at Thompson Brothers in Katanning as the chief machinist in their woodworking factory.

I cleared away the morning tea things and washed up in their kitchen sink. There was a tap protruding from the wall and when the handle was turned, out flowed some water. Our water used to be carted inside by bucket. The sink had a plug that when pulled would allow the water to drain away to the outside. Our old washing up dish was emptied into a drum by the back door so the water could be used for the vegie garden. The tea towel which I used was clean linen not the old raggedy cloth which I was used to. The cupboard that stored the crockery had a door on it which closed and was locked with a little wooden latch. It would be much better at keeping the mice away from the eating utensils.

There were a few little round boxes on some of the walls and as I was looking closely at one, Mr. Gomm came to stand beside me and operated the little lever that protruded from the little box. I was amazed that the light which hung from the ceiling began to glow and presently the room was bathed in light. Electric power was connected to most of the houses in Katanning as well as reticulated scheme water. They seem to live in such luxury. Our old kerosene lamps were smoky, smelly and always seemed to need refilling.

Mrs Gomm explained how she worked in her kitchen which was a feat in itself because she had such a difficulty in getting around. I could see that working in this kitchen with this lovely lady was going to be enjoyable.

I prepared the evening meal from left-overs from the icebox and when we had finished I quickly did the dishes and we all retired to the sitting room where there was an easy chair for each of us. They are so comfortable to sit in and very relaxing too. Mr. Gomm read aloud from his Bible while Mrs. Gomm's hands were busy with her crocheting. That was something that I had heard of but never seen done before but she promised that she would soon show me how to perfect the art.

I was tired that first day and I think I was asleep in the comfortable bed at about the same time that my head contacted the pillow.

My daily routine was laid out for me the next morning. I was late at waking and Mr. Gomm had already left for work but Mrs Gomm let me sleep as she thought that I needed the rest. I was a bit embarrassed at having stayed in bed for so long. It was already seven and I am usually out of bed long before this time but tomorrow will be better.

Mrs. Gomm told me to refer to her as Mummy and I have called her in that manner ever since that time. It seems like it has been many years since Mother passed away and as I felt so comfortable in Mrs Gomm's presence I thought that yes, she could be my mummy. After we had finished breakfast, she read a passage from the Bible as she does every morning. Mr. Gomm or Pop, as I was to refer to him, reads a different passage from the Bible after breakfast but I did miss out that first morning.

I could lay in bed until five thirty (there is a clock by my bed) then light the kitchen fire and prepare breakfast. Usually this is oatmeal porridge but on Saturday mornings it is eggs on toast and Pop likes his just cooked while Mummy prefers hers to be firm. That's so easy to cook for just three and in a good kitchen too. The big old cast iron frying pan hangs on a hook just above the wood stove so it's always warm to touch. The kettle is always on the stove so we can have a cuppa, without the wait for it to heat up.

Just as soon as breakfast is finished and the dishes done, I make the beds and sweep the house. The floor is only mopped on Friday unless it looks dirty before that. The dusting is done on Thursday mornings, so that leaves me quite a bit of free time but I soon learn how to crochet and knit so I am able to keep myself busy all day.

 I don't even need to bake bread as the local baker delivers twice a week right to the front door all for just 2 pence a loaf. Neither do I need to milk a cow anymore as the milkman delivers to the house each morning. All I have to remember to do is leave out the billycan with a note and the change for him each evening, so it's ready for him in the morning when he arrives with his horse and cart. I do try to meet him in the mornings so I can put the milk into the icebox straight away.

Pop and Mummy are very busy within the community. Pop's job at Thompson Brothers as chief machinist in their wood working factory keeps him in touch with so many people. They are very staunch Baptist Church members and he is a Lay preacher each Sunday, usually at churches in outlying districts. They also teach Sunday school to the younger ones and this is where I first met them so many years ago. I attend with them each Sunday and help with teaching the younger ones in their Sunday school lessons. I find it so rewarding and I also learn so much about the Bible and the Christian teachings that help us through our daily lives. Quite often we have a Bible study group on a weeknight. Sometimes we visit other people's homes for this Bible study and I get to know so many of the townsfolk.

Mummy is always busy with her hands and she has a little display of her handiwork for sale. She calls it her "Mission Box". The money which she raises from the sale of her pretty items is sent to the missions to help with their work, usually amongst those suffering from leprosy.

She has such a collection of hand sewn handkerchiefs, doylies, supper cloths and pillowslips. They all have a lot of designs sewn by her. She is so clever with her hands and I can only hope that I could be that clever one day too.

It is not long before I learn how to do her fine stitching and soon I am helping her with the handicraft too. She shows me so many different knitting stitches and soon I am knitting some clothes as well. I mentioned to her how we had made our own gowns for Dorothy's wedding and she was happy to know that I had had that experience.

Mummy chattered away while she was busy with her handiwork and she got around to the subject of England and where they came from before immigrating to Australia. Mummy was born in a small cottage called

Holmleigh in England. I think it was on the Isle of Wight.

This information started me to remember some the things which Mother had told us about the younger days and where she was brought up. I remember her telling us that her father had died at sea and that her mother was running the pub in Southampton called the "King's Arms" which was on High Street. Her mother remarried after grandfather's death. This time to a farmer. Her mother, sister and she moved to live on their farm which was close to town.

In years gone by Father was employed by one of the drapers in the town of Southampton and he was off very early each morning, taking orders from the newly arrived ships, so they could make new clothes for the sailors before they departed that night or when the tide was right. He came home around midday and was off again in the afternoon but usually didn't get home again until well after dark as he was delivering the new clothes to the sailors down at the harbour. Mother worked for the same firm and this is where they met.

It was fortunate that Dorothy and Florrie would visit from time to time and once or twice even stay the night with us, when they were able to get to town. They also filled in a lot of blanks about our families in our discussions around the table.

Chapter 4

From Dorothy and Florrie's visits I remember what they told me as I was so interested in our family's past.

I'll work on Father's side of the family first so that I don't get confused.

The earliest information that we know is that way back late in Roman times a couple of Lavisse boys left south of Italy as we know it today and travelled north looking for their opportunity to settle down away from the tyranny and oppression of the Roman Empire. They travelled for some years, north through Germany but were not able to find that special place for which they were seeking.

They then travelled south into France and eventually settled onto some land which they purchased in the very picturesque area to the northeast of Paris in the Champagne district. Rheims was their closest town. The main crop in the district is grapes which were grown for use in wine making but there were also flocks of sheep and herds of cattle grazing in the lush green pastures. Because of their Christian beliefs and their connection with the Huguenot society they did not grow grapes for wine production because they believed that wine was the "drink of the devil himself" and brought disease and destruction to those who over imbibed. But they did very well at raising cattle for milk and meat, sheep for their wool and meat and grew grain crops for milling into flour for bread. However their Huguenot religious connections caused them much trouble in a Catholic France and although they practiced their religion privately they still adhered to their Calvinistic beliefs. They worked very hard, became very prosperous and built up their holdings over many years and generations. They married into the local community and their families grew. Because there were four sons in the first generation, the property expanded to accommodate them. During the third generation the old house was rebuilt into a chateau which was quite appropriate for the district at that time. Each of the son's families grew and soon they had very large holdings in that part of the country.

As the family grew their requirements for more land became evident. One of the sons took his family south to find another opportunity. They found what they were looking for just out of the township of Nantes. An old estate which had fallen into disrepair as the old owner had died and left no family to carry on. Soon this land was productive again and after several generations the landholdings had increased along with the necessary help to operate the property.

Their lands incorporated several villages and from these they found their workforce for their dairies and on their farms, the holdings became so large. The men would work alongside their employees and the women were always busy with the women staff. They were well respected by their staff and village people.

The King became aware of the wealth which was generated by the family and he befriended them and became to learn that some of their philosophies were very similar to his own so he became an occasional visitor. Several generations of the family enjoyed the status that was bestowed on them by the successive Kings and they were referred to as Dukes. We don't know if they held any official titles in the King's court but they were certainly referred to in this way.

Being amongst the more wealthy members of the French population also drew the attention of other people as well. There was growing concern that the wealthy were taking advantage of the peasants forcing them to exist on subsistence income and not allowing them to work their way into a better station in life. The Lavisse family were very community minded and the families helped to care for the elderly, infirm and the needy within their workers' villages. Their Christian views were such that this was their way of doing God's work.

Frequently they would help with the cost of funerals for the departed. They worked with the sick and the ill to help them recover. They made sure that the children were able to have the education which was available at the time.

Now we advance the time to the early days of the French Revolution in the early 1790's, when due to several bad seasons, food was at a shortage and the prices forced many to starve. They had to make some very difficult decisions about letting some of their workers go as the crops failed to produce the grain or fodder that they should and the stock did not grow as they should. Production of all of their commodities was down but they delved into their reserves as much as possible to keep on as many of their staff as they could. But still it was difficult to make the decision to let some go.

I won't go into all of the details of the French Revolution but suffice it to say that the Lavisse family, as they were known in France, was on the hit-list of the revolutionaries.

The elders of the family decided that they would stay with the estates which they held and several of the younger families would escape to England where they would be able to live safely. This was a terrible decision and for many reasons. One of these being that who would be able to organise the workforce to produce the food that was so badly needed by the population.

It became a decision which each of them had to make with regards to their own and their immediate family's safety. If they stayed they risked the chance of losing their lands and having their heads chopped off by the revolutionaries or do they evacuated to the shores of England and save their necks but lose their lands.

However it turns out that although two of the families did in fact evacuate to England, probably from the Nantes area, the others attempted to stay but unfortunately suffered the demise of the loss of their lands and the loss of their heads as they were deemed to be part of the problem which caused France to be in the sad state of affairs in which it found itself.

Once the management of the land had ceased by the family, it would have taken many, many years before the production of meat, milk and grain would reach the production levels of previous because the people did not have the capital or the necessary skills to manage the farming operations.

It was around the early 1800's that the name of John Lavis is recorded in Devon, south west of London in England. From this we can ascertain that he was one of our family who was able to escape from the hands of the murderous revolutionaries in France. It seems that all of the property which was left in France was forfeited and registered with the French Chancery and now owned by the people.

His family is all that remains of a long line of our family who once lived in France, about which we know.

John (I) Lavis as he now called himself and his wife, Sally *(nee Holway)*, settled in Devon. They had several children one of the lads was also named John (II) after his father. When he was old enough he worked with his father who was an astute farmer and business man and learnt all he could from him.

John (II) became married to Elizabeth Mary Ann More in 1836 and between them they had two sons and four daughters.

It seems that our family has the fortune or misfortune to be able to move around a lot, looking for the ideal place in which to settle. This moving around has been going on for many generations and still continues to this day. Perhaps we are still looking for our ideal locale or perhaps we are not satisfied with what we have and are attempting to improve our lot. I don't know.

John (II) was a very astute business man in his own right, having learnt so much from his father and during his lifetime assembled a portfolio of many properties, several of these were farms where he raised sheep and horses. He developed a trade in horses with traders in Spain. These properties were left to his surviving family upon his death.

My great grandfather was William Henry Lavis, the second son of John (II). He received from his father, as mentioned above, several properties of land in Fulham. He later sold some of these properties and held a shop in Torquay and then a hair dressing establishment in Nottingham.

He had acquired the skills in hairdressing, wig making, perfumery and all of the sundry activities that complete that style of business operation. He is accounted as having several of the Royal household attend his premises for their own purchases.

William Henry was busy in the local community too and held several positions in the local church. The Baptist faith was the closest they could agree with as they made the changes from the Calvinists or the Huguenot faith. They worked with several of the charities that the Church favoured and developed good standing within the community.

William Henry became married to Lydia Walker in 1866 and they had three daughters, twin sons and Walter Dudley Lavis in 1878, who was to become my father. At this time they lived in Torquay, where grandfather, William Henry, operated his own hairdressing shop. By 1889 they had sold up from Torquay and moved to the new premises in Market Place, which is a suburb of Nottingham. It was here that grandfather continued his hairdressing, wig making, stationary and perfumery shop. They made their home not far from the shop in Melborn Street, Nottingham. My father was about twelve years old at this time. Grandfather later sold this shop and returned to Fulham where he had retained one of his properties.

My father began working for a company of seafaring clothing suppliers. He would take orders from the docks early in the morning and the factory workers would make the clothes and he would deliver them back to the ship before they sailed later that night or early the next morning. Firstly he worked out of the Tilbury Docks near London but later he moved to Southampton and worked for a similar firm there.

It was while he was living and working in Southampton, that he met my mother.

Chapter 5

I did so enjoy the times which Florrie and Dorothy
could visit me in the home of the Gomm's in Katanning.
Perhaps because I was so interested in what they had to
say about our family's history that made me so
enthralled but I certainly enjoyed that time.

The history of my mother's family is equally as
interesting and even some scandal too, but we'll come to
that shortly. Dorothy told me many of the details of our
grandmother's family and we'll have a look at the
details that I remember of that side of the family next.

It seems that the Burn family originates from Scotland
through a well-known poet by the name of Robby Burn.
During his time on God's earth, amongst many other
things, he settled in England. One of his descending
sons, William, married his sweetheart by the name of
Sarah. They had three daughters and three sons. The
youngest, a son was named George Frederick but he
had the nickname of John.

He worked his way around the sea ports and ships and
developed his skills until he became captain of his ship.
We don't know very much about this man who was my
grandfather. Records show that he died at sea when his
ship ran aground on a reef during a hurricane. But
before this calamity he had married a young lady by the
name of Mary Anne Pitt, who was the granddaughter of
Mr William Pitt, the Earl of Chatham. The Earl of

Chatham was Prime Minister of England for a time between 1766 and 1768.

Shortly after the marriage, George Frederick and Mary Ann settled down to run the King's Arms pub in High Street, Southampton. He spent a lot of time at sea but they had two daughters. The eldest, Alice Emily was my mother. Her younger sister was named Eliza Juliet. When grandfather died at sea, my mum, who was nicknamed "Doll" was five years old and Eliza whose nickname was "Lill" was just 2 years old. After the news arrived that grandfather had passed away they were devastated but still kept on at the King's Arms. About a year or so later, grandmother again became married. This time to a farmer by the name of William Hendry. Everyone moved from the pub to live in the home which was new to them. Over the next five years they gave my mum two step brothers and two step sisters to share their home with them.

Mother often recounted some of the events which she remembered as a child and teenager growing up on the farm. The animals and crops took more of their attention than feeding themselves and often the table was almost empty at meal times. However they did survive but I do think that their health may have suffered and this became evident in Mother's later years. Her experience on the family farm may have given father some help when he began farming later on.

Mother was very good with her hands and sewing and knitting were several of the skills which she mastered at an early age. As a teenager she was indented to a draper in Southampton who was, amongst other things, making clothing for the sailors who were visiting the local wharf. She enjoyed the work at the drapery and was employed there for many years. Her workmates were good to her and eventually introduced her to another of the workforce who was collecting the orders for the making of the sailor's clothing.

His name was Walter Dudley Lavis.

After working together for some time they became engaged and on 25th December 1901 they became married and lived in Southampton for a time.

Before Dorothy, their first child, arrived they moved to be closer to father's family in Greys which is a suburb of Essex to the east of London.

Leaving her family was very difficult for Mother and she did not fit in very well with father's family. She said that they were always "grumpy". But father wanted to be near his family and return to the place where he had worked before leaving to go to Southampton about ten years previous.

Mother kept house while Father continued with his work as a draper. He now collects his orders from the docks at Tilbury which is close to where they were living with grandfather. He takes these orders back to the factory where the garments are made up and he then delivers them back to the ships before they set sail again.

After a few encounters with some rough men on one of these trips to and from the docks, he acquired a pistol to carry in his pocket for his own protection. He never had to use it but it probably gave him a sense of security. Mother was not very happy with this arrangement and they had words over it. But father continued to carry the pistol and it passed into Florrie's care after he passed away, so many years later.

Mother presented Father with four children over the seven years while they lived with grandfather in Essex. Dorothy was born in 1904, Florrie in 1905 and Ray in 1908. But not everything went to plan. Baby Stanley died from complications from a convulsive attack and was laid to rest. Mother was devastated by this tragic situation and it took many months before she began to feel her old self again. She had tried everything which she knew to help her poor baby. She even had her mother-in-law assist her too but still they were not able to prevent his death. The doctor was summoned but he was busy elsewhere and was not able to attend in time. He did arrive but not in time to save poor little Stanley. Ray too had his problems. A growth appeared on one of his eyes just like a cloud over the pupil. When it didn't clear up after a week or so whilst under the doctor's direction, he was admitted to hospital and the eye was removed. It was marvellous what they did in those days of medical development as they made a glass eye for him and it looked quite real. He was just a small child when that happened.

Mother's health too, suffered badly after the events of losing her baby and Ray's problem. Today it would probably be called depression but in those day it would have been called "melancholia". Father was experiencing health problems himself and it was suggested to him that perhaps a warmer climate would be more suited to both his and mother's health.

Father discussed his situation of travel to Australia with several seaman whom he was visiting and they suggested that he should talk to one of the captains. This he did and after some months of deliberation he set off in the "Otranto" on the fifteenth of September, 1909, bound for Sydney. Mother had arranged to travel later on another ship. This was to give Father time to purchase a property in Australia onto which they could settle and begin a new life of farming.

He had previously spent some time with his grandfather and uncles on their farms and quite liked the idea. He enjoyed the work with the horses and lent a hand when it came time to maintain the equipment and machinery. He liked the lifestyle where they could take days off from their farms and the farm workers would take care of things while they were away. He could just see himself in that situation but not in England. He read some details about the drawcard of life on the land in

Australia and liked what he saw and read. The price of land, particularly in Western Australia, was very appealing to him and probably was one of the main reasons for his selection. At 15 to 30 shillings per acre, he thought the price was very appealing.

He felt that he should find a new direction for his and his family's life and he felt that he could best do this in Australia.

But farming in Australia is very different from farming in England as Father was to find out. He travelled as ship's crew to Sydney and then returned to Fremantle and on to Katanning where he purchased his land. Mother, along with my sisters Dorothy and Florrie and my brother, Ray left on the "Orsova" on the fifth of February 1910 bound for Fremantle.

The trip was interrupted as they passed through the Suez Canal as Dorothy had developed scarlet fever and the ship's captain made them disembark and get treatment in a Port Said hospital. After about six weeks they resumed their trip but this time aboard the "Omrah".

Father wasn't aware at the time of his departure that mother was carrying her fifth child so when he received a letter from Mother, he was overjoyed and surprised. Baby Don was born in the sick bay of the Omrah and the ship's crew suggested that he should be named after the ship. So he was named Donald Omrah Lavis and was born just a few days before the ship reached the port of Fremantle.

Because of the delay, Father wasn't at the ship to greet mother and the children so they stayed for several nights in accommodation, until father could collect them and return to Katanning on the steam train passenger service. She was beginning to experience the new climate and conditions in their new country.

She was shocked at the condition of the house which was to be their home. It was "so last century".

Life in their new country continued but not always to their benefit. Conditions were extremely harsh and Father with no real knowledge of farming, particularly in this new country, certainly did not help. He took jobs working for other farmers to gain experience but it took him a long time to understand that things are so much different in Australia than they were in England. Farm labour was very expensive or not available at all and anything which needed to be done or build had to be done by Father. So progress was very slow.

But life continues as they progress through droughts, floods, hot summer temperatures and pleasant winters, poor crops, good crops and sick animals.

Chapter 6

Life with the Gomm's in their Katanning home continued to be one of the most pleasant experiences of my life to that time.

Church on Sundays was the pinnacle of the week. I was helping with teaching the younger children with their Sunday school lessons. We travelled around the district doing God's work which occasionally took us to Badgebup where I could catch up with my younger sisters and father. Unfortunately my step-mother was there too and she was still causing problems with us all. Pop Gomm heads off to work at Thompsons each morning at about seven and usually gets home again about five thirty just in time for the evening meal at six. He does have Sunday off with the rest of the workers, so he is able to spend some time with us.

He works with several others in the factory and one day they were pushing a piece of timber through the saw when a large splinter punctured his arm near the wrist and exited just below the elbow. The workers were able to rush him to the Katanning Hospital and the splinter was removed in surgery. There was damage to the muscles of his arm but the bones were not harmed. The operation did leave a nasty looking scar where the skin had to be cut to remove the splinter. He didn't keep the splinter as a memento but he does joke about that from time to time. But the scar on his arm was with him for the rest of his life. The muscle damage restricted the movement of his arm and it took some time with frequent doctor's visits for it to heal but he would not return to the factory to work. The accident happened during February in 1930.

Now that Pop was not able to return to work at Thompson's factory, where he had been the head machinist, he began looking for something else for himself to do. He was a busy man and sitting still was not in his nature. He had the need to occupy his time to the fullest.

It was during this time when he wasn't able to work that he and Mummy told me of their background. They had listened earnestly to the discussions which I had had with Dorothy and Florrie about our family's backgrounds and he was so surprised that there was so many similarities with their family history too. He was born in Southampton in 1872. Mummy was born as Mary Ruth Jotham in 1870 in Southampton. Their daughter, Clarice Lillian was born in Southampton but their son, Leslie Jotham was born on the Isle of Wight which is near Southampton. They lived on the Isle of Wight for several years before they immigrated to Australia aboard the "Omrah" in 1905.

Mummy's parents were living in Western Australia too, so this helped them to choose that location. Her mother Francis, passed away while she was living at Bridgetown in December 1915.

Pop was an experienced wood machinist and when they arrived in Western Australia they lived at Baronia which is now Mount Helena and he worked at the Lion Mill where the company he worked for was making equipment for the railways. During their stay at Baronia their daughter was married to Walter Arnott in Mundaring. When Pop's contract finished with Lion Mill, they made the move to Katanning where he worked for Thompsons in their factory.

Now that he was unable to work at his profession, Pop frequently scoured the newspapers and eventually found a small poultry farm which was for sale in Armadale which appeared to suit his purpose.

He visited Armadale by train to look at the property and business before he made up his mind to make the move.

Once he decided to go ahead with the deal, we took a week or so to tidy up our affairs in Katanning.

We were able to get hold of a number of plywood tea-chests and into these we packed all of the household goods with the exception of the larger furniture. A truck arrived and everything was loaded up and delivered to the railway station then loaded onto the train for the trip to the new home.

The local community and my family came together to put on a valedictory and supper that was so enjoyable. It was held in the Baptist Church Hall which was prettily decorated by the ladies. The Rev. F Potter led the proceedings and there were also speeches by Mr Law-Davis. So many people spoke on the evening and they all spoke well of Pop for his work in the local community and Church. I remember Mr Law-Davis spoke of Pop as "a consistent Christian between Sundays". I thought that was certainly very fitting for my new friends. After the singing of a few hymns, we had a fine supper to close off the evening.

I probably was not going to see my father or sisters very often from now on, so this gave me the chance to say my goodbyes. I would miss them so much but living with the Gomm's would make up for some of the disappointment.

By the end of April 1930, we were ready to make the move to Armadale. We boarded the train and waving goodbye to those who came to see us off at the platform we began our journey.

Chapter 7

The poultry farm was in Fifth Road, Armadale and it was accompanied with a comfortable house. It didn't take us long to get our furniture and other goods unpacked and make the house into our home.

Pop had a man helping with the poultry work and I was kept busy in the house looking after Mummy. The eggs needed to be carted into the markets in Subiaco but on the way to the markets he was able to sell some of his eggs to several of the shops which lined the road which he took. He could make a better return for selling direct to these shops but they were only able to take a small percentage of his production, so most of the eggs went to the markets in Subiaco.

The old horse which had served Pop so well for so many years was left behind in Katanning and now he bought a Chevrolet van. He tells me all about it from time to time but I was not very mechanically minded it didn't seem to register with me. But it did have four cylinders and was 25 horsepower. It had wooden spokes on the front wheels and steel rims at the back and rubber tyres all round. The doors came halfway up the side of the cabin and it was great in the summer as the breeze could just blow right through. The windscreen kept out the wind as we drive along and prevents most of the rain for making us wet.

But the winter breeze was a bit colder and not quite so comfortable and when it rained heavy with a side wind behind the rain, it came straight inside and we got wet. Now, don't get me wrong, I'm not complaining! With the horse and buggy you got wet right through even with a light shower of rain. So this was so much better. During the weekday evenings we all went into the Baptist church in Armadale and attended the local Christian Endeavour Group. We had a wonderful time with these people and made some very lasting friends. We'd usually meet each Wednesday evening in the church hall and we'd all bring a plate for supper. We'd study the Bible for a while, sing a few hymns and have a general discussion before we began our supper. I thoroughly enjoyed my time with this group of friends. We had some special times particularly at the Harvest Festival service in spring. Everyone would bring along something which they grew or produced on their farm or in their garden and we would celebrate God's handy work and pray for a bountiful harvest. Even a few animals found their way into the church but it certainly wasn't the place for horses or cows but Pop did bring in one of his hens along with a pack of eggs. I had a garden just behind the house and grew some corn, strawberries, beetroot, carrots and grapes. A few of these found their way into a basket which Mummy and I took along. Dorothy invited me down to their home. Abel and she have the mixed farm called "Passchendaele" not far out of Katanning. Her twins were to be celebrating their second birthday and she so badly wanted to see me and I so badly wanted to catch up with them and her twin daughters again. I took the opportunity to visit Father too. Only Connie and Margaret were at home. Chrissie and the twins were working out on different farms helping keep house for other families or as nannies for their children. I was so disappointed to miss seeing them on this trip. Hopefully I will see them again before too long.

Our Christmas services in the Church were wonderful too. And we all enjoyed singing the Christmas Carols as well. It was times like this that I missed the girls and Father but we did write and receive cards from them too.

In July 1932, Mummy became ill and the doctors moved her into hospital where she could be better cared for. I had looked after her for the last three years but the doctor says that this illness is different from what she was suffering from before. Then it was a problem with her hip and knee which is why she had so much difficulty in moving around but now it seems that cancer has invaded her system and she became very ill quite quickly. Pop and I would visit her in hospital as soon as our chores were finished and we'd take turns at sitting with her for as long as we could. Mummy's health deteriorated very quickly and early in August 1932 she passed away. It was a very sad occasion as she had been my friend for years. She meant so much to me. Mummy had taught me so much about how to keep myself busy with doing things and more about myself. She had been a true friend and was going to be very sadly missed.

Her funeral service was held at the Baptist Cemetery in Karrakatta on the Tuesday following her death from 4:15 in the afternoon. Pop and I travelled to Smith and Co, the undertakers, in Newcastle Street with their son Les Gomm, in his car. From there we travelled in the cortege to the funeral service. It was such a solemn affair as most funeral services are but everyone from the Armadale Christian Endeavour group attended.

The next few weeks were hard for us to adjust to the new household arrangements. I'd always been up first to light the fire and get things ready for breakfast and I kept on laying the table with a place for her to sit at. Then I would sit and cry quietly for a few minutes. But I would make sure that my eyes were dried before Pop would sit at the table for breakfast. He would always say grace before the meal and now it seemed to take on a different meaning with Mummy gone. She may be gone from our home but she will never be gone from our hearts. The Bible readings after the meal also seemed to have a deeper meaning and a few times I could see him struggling too but he was too much of a gentleman to break down, in front of me at least.

As the weeks progressed the pain of her passing diminished and we returned to a more normal life. Our connection with the Church and the Christian Endeavour group certainly were a great help over the next month or so. Their understanding, care and friendship means so much, particularly at a time like this.

Life eventually became a new sort of normal with Pop taking his eggs to the markets and usually coming home with some little things special for the table. A small ham for our Christmas dinner was a blessing. The occasional bar of chocolate we could share after our dinner at night was special.

The next big event that the Christian Endeavour group helped me so much with was my twenty first birthday party, which was on the twenty seventh of August 1933. Several others of the group had celebrated their "Turning of Age" with their families but mine was so far away and the cost of travel was so high that they were unable to attend. I was so disappointed about this but I did understand. Pop made a key from a piece of wooden packing box and polished it up for me. This was presented to me with a pretty pink ribbon attached. I only forgot to have everyone who was there to sign it for me but I did engrave it by hand afterwards. I still have that key today.

The Christian Endeavour group is expanding with more young people getting together to share their experiences and love of God. There is even a couple of lads who cycle in from as far away as Keysbrook. They attend a couple of times a month and fit into the group very well. They certainly are very fit as they are dairy and orchard farmers and start work, well before sunrise. So after cycling home again they must only just get a few hours' sleep after the meeting, before they need to rise again for their days' work.

They are both very handsome but I seem to take a shine to the older of the two boys and get to know that his name is Lance Kentish. His younger brother is Clem and they work on the family farm with their father and sister.

One evening as everyone else was leaving the hall we took a walk together and we talked about our families and what we had been up to in recent years. It was great to be with him and talk in a friendly and open way. I think I may have shared some of my secrets with him too and he was most understanding. I certainly look forward to when he could get to our meetings. Because of his work on the farm it was difficult to get enough time to make the trip very often. But we did get to see each other every couple of months. He is also the secretary of the Primary Producers Association and that also takes some of his time.

These warm summer nights under the starry sky must have been to our advantage as when he went down on bended knee and asked me to marry him and be his bride.

I immediately said "YES!"

That was such a lovely evening. That's a date I'll always remember, the fifteenth of February 1934.

Well, I'm sure my feet were off the ground for the next few days. It felt like I was walking on air, I was so happy. Fancy me from my background finding such a wonderful man who works so hard.

Lance and Clem along with their sisters Enid and Esther attended meetings of the Young People's Club in North Dandalup. This is a similar group to the Christian Endeavour group that we belong to in Armadale.

The next thing is for me to meet his family. This was arranged when a group of us would visit the Young People's Club in North Dandalup in a few months' time. I was a bit apprehensive when the day arrived. Pop and I drove down to North Dandalup in his Chev van and after the meeting we are to stay at the Kentish home overnight. This would give me a chance to meet with them for the first time. There are so many at the meeting and their structure is very similar to our own Christian Endeavour group. We read and study the Bible and discuss ways that the teachings there can be best applied to modern day life. After about an hour they pause their meeting and elect a new Vice President as the old one had moved away from the district. There were a number of nominations but the vote went to

Lance. His duties may be minor but he is held in such high esteem and that shows by the confidence that everyone else has in him. The evening concluded with the usual cup of tea, cake and scones. The cream was brought by Esther, Lance's sister and it was the richest fresh cream I had ever tasted. Esther was lovely and very energetic while Enid was more reserved and quiet but she did play the piano very well.

Time was getting away from us and Pop decided we should depart and head to the Kentish farm before it was too late, as the rest of the family wanted to greet Pop and I. Lance and his group drove home in their baby Austin car and Pop and I drove off in his van. My palms were sweating as we approached the farm and Pop said some kind words to calm me down as I was extremely nervous at the prospect of meeting Lance's parents.

Lance's dad was a slightly stooped man with a beard and the largest hands I had ever seen. His mum was lovely and we all hit it off straight away. Pop told them what I was doing for his wife and said that I was welcome to stay with him until we became married. We stayed that night and slept on the verandah as it was still very warm. When we got out of our beds in the morning, everyone was up and heading off to the dairy to milk the cows. We declined the offer to watch as Pop needed to get back to his chooks. We said our goodbyes and drove back to Armadale.

A few months after that day Pop sold his poultry farm and bought a fruit shop in Subiaco. Soon we moved into the accommodation section of the shop which was situated at 391 Hay Street. The shop was very busy. Pop had made several good friends at the markets as he had been delivering his eggs there for the past several years. So he would visit there each morning and buy the vegetables and fruit for the day's trade.

Molly had an operation in Katanning hospital for appendicitis so she finished her job with the family just out of Katanning and travelled all the way to Perth on the train. The doctors had told her to convalesce and I met her at the station and after such a wonderfully warm greeting we set off on the train to Subiaco. We slowly walked the rest of the way. It was uphill but still only took us several minutes. Molly was talking excitedly the whole time as we had such a lot to catch up on. I looked after her for several days as she became stronger. A month or so and she was again back on deck.

Pop gave me a couple of hours off from my normal shop duties and Molly and I spent that time just talking and catching up with the news from home. She had brought me a letter from Father in which he congratulated me on my engagement and wish us all the very best for our future together. He said that if I loved Lance as much as he had loved Mother we would have a happy life together. Well this did bring tears to my eyes as I remembered Mother but also the remarks were unexpected from Father.

Life gets back to normal for a while with Molly and me working with Pop in his shop. He had a contract to supply fresh vegetables to the men who were constructing the Canning Dam. I remember after he had come back from the markets we filled the order and loaded all of the fruit and vegies into the Chev and drove up the hill to where the construction team had their meals. The causeway crosses over the Swan River and the planks which form the top of the bridge used to rattle as we crossed over. Pop used to remark each time that it happened that "I hope that's the bridge making that noise and not the spokes in our front wheels". We both laughed at the joke. It did make such a clatter.

Chapter 8

Moly and I received an invitation to attend Chrissie's wedding which was to be held in September 1935. She had been courted by Ron Hewson and they are going to be married next month and she would like it very much if we could be there. Well, we certainly would not miss the chance to be there and share her special day. Molly knew about this before and she was to be a bridesmaid at the wedding. She and I had been spending many nights making our own dresses and we were happy that we would look grand in them too. Molly and I took the train from Subiaco Station and changed trains at Perth Station. Here we travel up to Clackline and then on the Great Southern Line, which runs through Spencer's Brook, York, Beverly, Brookton, Narrogin, Wagin and then we disembark after the train arrives at Katanning. It was a very tiring day and we were glad to see a friendly face at the station when we arrived. Abel Austin was there and after putting our luggage in the back, off we drove to his and Dorothy's place where we were to stay.

Dorothy's twins were now about two years old and it was great to see those little ones again.

Chris and Ron's wedding was such a lovely event in the Church in town and then we all went back to Florrie and Harold's farm called "Hillside" for the reception. Florrie had done such a marvellous job of setting up the room and providing such a great fare for the wedding breakfast. It was late by the time we returned to Dorothy's that night and I think we may have overslept the next morning.

But it was great to catch up with the girls as they were able to get time off from their situations and spend a little time with the family. They were all excited and always asking about Lance and the farm which they worked at Keysbrook.

The trip back to Subiaco seemed to take forever. The train seemed to be going ever so slow but we did finally arrive home just before dark.

During the autumn, Molly had a young man come into the shop one day and he began a conversation with her. Pop and I stood well back as they seemed to be having a very private discussion. He came in several times and then they went to several dances at the Church hall. It wasn't long before they became engaged. Molly and Jim Stewart planned their wedding for the end of November 1936.

In June 1936 we received a letter from Katanning. It was sent by Myrtle who was so excitedly writing to tell us that she had become engaged to Len Pember from Gnowangerup. She enclosed a cutting from the local paper with the details. She also wrote that to expect an invitation to the wedding which was planned for early November 1936.

It seems that everyone in our family is moving on to the next part of our exciting lives.

Yes we did get to Myrtle and Lens' wedding and it was a great chance to see them all again. But the long and arduous train travel was becoming a bit of a bore. But it was worth the difficulty just to catch up with the family again.

Molly and Jim's wedding later in November 1936 was also a lovely affair. The West Leederville Baptist church is where we visit each Sunday for our devotions and church service, so it was very familiar to us. The ladies of the congregation have decorated the church with some lovely flowers and it does look a picture as we walk in. Reverend Holly married Molly and Jim in his usual flourishing manner and they lived in Claremont. Jim was to later join the army, became sergeant and had a long service both in Australia and New Guinea where he spent the latter part of his service time.

Together they had four boys with two of them being twins. Which is rather ironic as Molly was one of a set of twins.

It's just a few months until Lance and I get married and Pop said that the excitement is beginning to show. He says he can see it in the way I do things. Just some little subtle changes.

Lance's parents have invited Pop and myself to their home to share in our Christmas celebrations this year. How wonderful will that be? It will give me a chance to meet them properly as we have been so busy lately with the shop being busy and Pop delivering the fruit and vegie to the Canning dam construction crew.

After attending to the closing of business on Christmas Eve we set out for Keysbrook, arriving just on dark. The milking had just been completed, so we were able to meet everyone at the house. We spend some time getting to know Lance's mum, while the others are washing up and readying themselves for the evening meal. The smell from the roast mutton in the oven wafts over us as we talk in the kitchen. There's another pot on the wood fired stove top that's bubbling merrily away. Fresh beans, I suppose from the garden which is out behind the wash-house. We saw it as we came in. It is quite extensive as you would expect, to able to feed a hard working family of six.

They are such a lovely family and Pop and I fit in well with their activities. Being Christian folks like us they say grace prior to the meal and read from the Bible after the meals are completed. Esther jumps up and gets her hands into the dish water as soon as she can. It looks like she enjoys the work. Mrs Kentish suggests that I might like to join the men on the verandah for a chat and she'll be there shortly. Enid takes this time to sit at the piano and play some lovely music for us. She seems so adept at the piano.

Lance and I are discussing our wedding and honeymoon plans. We have planned for a March thirteenth wedding. It will be a Saturday so it should suit most folks.

We sit around talking with Lance by my side and Pop not far away. When the others join us, Pop stands up and announces that he would like to say something. He goes on to tell them of how I have been helping with Mummy and how much he appreciates the work which I have done for him and he says that if the farm can provide the necessary items, he will build Lance and I a new house to live in as a wedding present. Well, this was news to me but I think he may have had this in mind for some time.

It will mean that Pop will need to sell his shop and move to Keysbrook. He would even build a room so he can stay with us as he needs. We all thanked him very much for his very kind gesture and Mrs Kentish said that we could all live at the main house until such time that the new house was ready for habitation.

Well, it seems like all of our prayers have been answered. Everything seems to be falling into place just nicely.

The men began discussing how they could obtain the timber and other hardware that would be needed. Pop has kept all his tools, so he won't need to borrow any. The discussion goes on well into the night but with it being Christmas Day tomorrow we soon all head off to sleep as tomorrow is going to be busier then usual.

Lance has Esther wake me before he leaves for the milking shed and after wishing me a Merry Christmas, asks me to join him so I can see them milking the seventy or so cows by hand. The cows all seem to be happy to walk into the bails, where they get some feed in a bin. Each cow is hand milked in about 4 minutes, so the four of them get all of the cows milked in nearly three hours. Esther milks at the same pace as the men folk and they all seem to be having a competition to see who can milk the cows fastest. It looks like Mr Kentish may not be the fastest today. Once each milk bucket is filled it is taken to the milk room where it is emptied into a large ten gallon can. These are stood in a trough of water to cool the milk. When the milking is finished the fourteen or fifteen cans are loaded onto a ramp and they will be picked up by a carrier during the morning and taken to the milk factory near the city. After the milking is finished the straw floor is cleaned with shovel and broom. As soon as that is completed, we all walk back to the house.

We all fit around the dining table and after grace we are presented with a large breakfast of bacon, eggs and sausages with toast by Mrs Kentish and Enid. I struggle to get through the meal as it is much larger than I have been used to. When we have all finished, Mr. Kentish reads some special passages from the Bible that talk about the Christmas event. Luke chapter 2 verses 10, 11,

13 to14 is one of my favourites along with John, chapter 3 verse16.

After the dishes have been completed we all adjourn to the lounge room where the Christmas tree is standing in the corner. Clem had cut a small native tree and set it into a bucket with sand. The girls have decorated the tree with handmade items which look very pretty. Silver and coloured paper wrapped around gumnuts do a great job as baubles. Silver paper over cardboard cut-out stars go very well too. It looks just like the ones which we used to have when we were children. We had so much fun then making all the decorations for our tree, so I imagine the girls have had their fun here too.

We unwrapped our gifts and enjoyed the time we had together. As we sit around talking and enjoying each other's company, Enid plays so many of our favourite tunes on the piano. Eventually we break out singing to the tunes which Enid is playing and we have a very enjoyable time.

Christmas lunch is a splendid affair with baked vegies which were growing in their garden yesterday. A roast of mutton, roasted duck and chicken with several different gravies. I help the women bring the dishes to the table and after grace we all enjoy this sumptuous meal together.

Lance and I take a walk while the other girls do the dishes and we talk about our wedding and the future that we will be sharing in a few months. Clem has

agreed to be Lance's best man and his cousin Keith
Nicholls as his groomsman. He suggested that perhaps
Esther might be one of my bridesmaids and this I agree
to. I tell him that now that Connie is working near the
city, I will ask her to be my bridesmaid too. It all seems
to be working out well. He is very impressed that Pop
will be building our new house. Lance suggests that the
farm could use a good man like him to do some of the
lighter work. There is always so much to do.
Later in the afternoon we say our goodbyes and we
drive back to Subiaco and get in just before dark.
The next few weeks are a blur but the last few days
leading up to our wedding were frantic. All those things
that I thought would just fall into place seem to be a
problem. But Connie and I have been busy with our
frocks which have been made by a family friend and
have overcome most of the difficulties. Esther has come
to town for a fitting too and all seems to be going well.
She even bought me a horseshoe for me to use. But it's a
bit big and heavy, so I think I'll go with the cut-out one I
had made before. I think Clem may have set her up. He
is a bit of a jokester.
Our day has come at last! Saturday the thirteenth of
March 1937.
Esther and Connie stayed with me at Pop's Hay Street
home for the night, so that we could help each other as
we prepare.

We washed and dried our hair and we each set the other. Connie's and mine are very dark while Esther's is a lighter colour, so we decide to keep our hair style quite simple.

We dress and then help each other with the finer points of our outfits. The two girls are wearing gowns made from a blue floral georgette and lined with white silk. They have a boat neck with puffy sleeves with a bow of the same material on the left shoulder. They are wearing white court shoes with a heel. On their heads we have arranged floral coronets which do look such a treat.

My dress is made from a cream crinkled silk with a vee neck and I wore three strands of pearls. My long veil is gathered to a coronet of orange blossom and embroidered around the edge. The short train just trails on the floor.

The horseshoe which I have embroided with gold ribbon, hangs from the bouquet which has fish fern mixed with maiden hair fern and small cream roses. The bouquet is tied with a sash with tassels at the ends. The girl's bouquet are very similar but just a little smaller.

The final touches had been added to our outfits when I walked into the lounge room to speak to Pop when the sleeve of my dress got caught on the door handle and tore. Oh bother! Now we'll need to fix that before we leave for the Church and we are already a little behind time. Connie quickly took a needle and thread and she worked feverishly to repair the damage. In five minutes the disaster was avoided and she did such a great job that you couldn't even see where the tear was.

Over the last few years, Pop and I have been attending the West Leederville Baptist Church. Lance and I decided some time ago that we would get married here. The church has been decorated by the ladies of the congregation who are such a lovely group of ladies too! They are always so willing to help.

As father is unable to attend our wedding, Pop was overjoyed to have the honour of walking me down the aisle. We arrived in a couple of friend's cars. The church is near full and as we walk down the aisle I see the faces of so many friends, new and older. Many from the Armadale Christian Endeavour group are here too. Lance with Clem and their cousin Keith Nicholls are standing by the alter watching as I draw near. The Reverend Strickson stands by them waiting for me to arrive.

I am so nervous, I'm sure Lance can see me shaking. After I reach them, Connie takes my bouquet from me and after handing it to Esther lifts the veil from my face. Rev. Strickson begins the ceremony and because my nerves never left me, all that was said during the ceremony was just a blur. The next thing I remember is Lance kissing me full on the lips and then we move into the vestry where we all sign the paperwork.

We walk hand in arm as we exit the church with all of the congregation showing their support for us. Outside the door, large handfuls of confetti showers over us and some of it sticks to our clothes.

Our reception was held in the Church Hall in Subiaco and it was a grand affair. The thirty friends all wished us well after the speeches were made. Lance and I then changed into our going away clothes and everyone cheered and wished us well as we walked out from the hall and got into the baby Austin car which Lance had ready for us.

Chapter 9

Now begins a new chapter to my life which
includes Lance.

After Lance has driven along the dirt road, taking
care to keep out of the many potholes, we arrive at
the Ravenswood Hotel just before dark. We are
surprised to be greeted by the owner, Mrs Amy
Thomas. Such a lovely lady and she showed us to
our room that was called "The Bridal Suite". A
young lad brings our two cases and we spend just a
few minutes hanging our clothes to let the creases
fall out. It seems Lance has the same respect for his
clothing as I do, so things should go well with us.
It's such a luxurious room to me but then it is also
the first hotel room in which I have stayed.

We take the evening meal in the restaurant, another
first for me and I think it was a first for Lance too.
The depression years have taught us to be very
frugal with our spending and even though this is
our honeymoon, it still seems extravagant. Fish of
the day with steamed vegies followed by steamed
pudding with custard and cream, was my selection
as I don't usually get to eat fish very often. We sat
and talked for a long time there before we retire to
our rooms.

The sunshine sneaks in through the window between the curtains in the morning. We had a wonderful time last night enjoying each other. We stay for a night or two and the relaxing time was wonderful. The little car takes us to several places and in Mandurah we watch the fishing boats as they enter the estuary and tie up at the rickety old jetty. We attend the church service in Pinjarra on the Sunday morning and meet several of the members from the North Dandalup Young Peoples group who were at the service too. Mr Doley was the minister, whom we met for the first time. We stay in Bunbury for a night or two and take in the sights of the town. The wharf areas and some of the dairies around the area are of special interest for Lance.

We enjoyed our four days out and about the areas but like all good things, our honeymoon soon came to an end. So after loading the car, we head to the Bolinda Vale farm at Keysbrook to begin our new life together.

We return back the way we have come from and then heading east from Ravenswood, Lance drives along some of the tracks which they use to travel to Mandurah for their beach-side holidays. There are a few swamps and a lot of paperbark trees and tea tree which join together overhead. Just like driving through a tunnel.

Presently the Keysbrook railway station blocks our track, so we must deviate and continue on the road up to where we meet the Bunbury road. The settlement of Keysbrook is here, with a post office, new hall, tennis courts and several houses.

We stop out the front and Lance takes me inside the post office and introduces me to Mrs Bee who runs the post office along with her small shop which has some of the basic items which one might need from time to time.

The Bunbury road which runs past Keysbrook and Bolinda Vale had recently been bituminised. It was a change from driving on tracks and roads which were much less comfortable. That poor little car was bouncing around all over the place on those other roads.

As we drive into the farm's driveway we meet the cartage contractor who has just delivered some timber for our house. It was so exciting to see so many changes so soon. It will be difficult to keep up with it all.

Lance sounds the horn on the little car as we pull up and as it is just before lunchtime, everyone is there to greet us and welcome me to their home. Well, it will be my home too for a while, until Pop has the new house finished.

Such a warm welcome too as we are all seated around the lunch table. Dad, as I am to call him, says grace and Mum, as I am to call her, dishes up the cold mutton and cold roasted vegies onto our plates. Clem, Enid and Esther are also at the table and we tell them of all the places we've been to and the things we have seen. Pop will join us in a few days as he is tidying up his affairs in Subiaco. The discussion soon gets around to dairy cows and some of the difficulties they are having with a problem called mastitis. This is a problem that is apparently very difficult to control and it is causing Dad some headaches in dealing with it. Lance tells them of a dairy which he visited on our honeymoon and made a few suggestions, so we'll see what becomes of that.

The girls have given us their bedroom as they mostly sleep on the verandah during the warmer months, so Lance and I have some privacy for ourselves.

The days begin early as I work alongside Esther and she shows me how they do things on this farm. The days are becoming shorter as summer develops into autumn and we begin our day at four thirty before the sun has risen but it is already light enough to see what we are doing.

Firstly we walk out to the back of the paddock and follow the cows in to the dairy. Some of them are a bit reluctant to move so early in the morning. I do sympathise with them as it is early for me too. We round them up and soon they are following the rest of the herd into the yard.

They have built a four stand milking shed as there are the four of them hand milking, so Esther shows me how to dish out the feed for the cows as they come into the bails to be milked. Each stand has a feed bin that I put a dipper full of gristed grain into. The cows seem to enjoy their breakfast as they munch away at the feed from their bin. Each time a cow has been milked she is let out of the bail and I follow her out to the back yard. As the next cow comes into the bail I put in some more feed. I have some spare time so I stand behind and watch them hand milking. They certainly are much faster that I remember that I was back on the family farm in Badgebup.

After about three hours all of the cows have been milked and they are waiting patiently to be let back out into their paddock once again. Esther and I follow them back to the paddock chasing up the few stragglers on the way. There always seems to be one or two who have a mind of their own, no matter how well they know what they are supposed to do. After the gate is locked, we join the men back at the dairy as they are cleaning up. The straw on the dirt floor is raked up and the dirty straw and manure put onto a pile out the back. Mum raids this pile of straw and manure for her garden when she thinks it need some attention. The cleaner straw is spread over the floor again and several new sheaves have their ties cut and are added as well.

The men take the cans of milk and put them into the water trough to keep them cool until the truck arrives to take them to the city where the milk is processed for distribution around the city.

We head for the house when this is all finished and we find that Mum has breakfast nearly ready for us. Homemade sausages with bacon and eggs with

toast from yesterday's bake on the side plate.
Before we begin to eat, Dad says grace, "Lord
accept our thanks for these and all of your mercies.
In Jesus' name, amen".

A very simple grace but complete in its simplicity
with its meaning.

After the meal, the boys lather jam on their toast
and cover it with fresh cream. A cup of tea with a
choice of milk or cream washed down the meal.
They certainly have an appetite.

Before we leave the table, Dad recites a prayer and
asks the Good Lord for guidance through the day
while protecting everyone. Mum reads a passage
from the Bible. She selects a different passage each
morning. One which suits the day's activities that
lie ahead.

Once our daily devotions are completed, the girls,
Mum and I collect the dishes and get the washing
up done in real quick time.

While we are doing this chore, Dad and the boys
are discussing their days work.

They have some more clearing to do. The property
which they purchased five years before across
Bunbury Road needs some more clearing and

fencing. They will be working there for the next few weeks until it's time to plant the crop for hay. They have a team of eight Clydesdale horses which they use for the clearing work. They use chains, axes, mattocks and crosscut saws to do the clearing. It is very heavy work.

The men head out and are working hard by eight thirty.

After we do a tub of hand washing and have it hanging on the line to dry, we make morning tea and take it out to the men in the paddock. Esther has a very quiet horse which is harnessed to a buggy and we are soon there with the men. We gather up some small firewood and soon have the billy boiling. The men must have been able to smell the boiling water, because just as the billy boiled they were sitting down on the ground waiting.

I have never seen a dozen scones, covered with so much jam and cream eaten so quickly. They have good manners but had the capacity to eat an awful lot. None of them had an ounce of fat on their bodies, they were working so hard and even at this early time of the day the sweat was heavy on them too.

They soon get back to work and after dowsing the fire, we climb onto the buggy and watch them at work for a while.

Those two men on the crosscut saw! The sawdust was flying and I had never seen one be used so fast. Lance did keep the teeth sharp and the speed at which it cut showed that.

Some of the logs were from jarrah trees and these were cut into six foot lengths and then split to make fence posts. The red gum trees were added to the heaps that would be burnt after the first rains. Apparently they don't make good fence posts.

We leave the men to their work and head back to the house, where we pick up a couple of boxes and continue on to the orchard to pick some fruit. The apples and pears are ripe and we soon have several boxes filled. Mum sorts these and sends them off to fill her orders for as far away as Kalgoorlie. There are many varieties of fruit trees here and many of them are only young but will have fruit on them next season.

Some of the fruit which is unsuitable for sale we either put on our table or feed them to the pigs. The pig sty is only small and has two sows which have little ones running around. They are so much fun just to sit and watch. Not that there is much of that, we seem to be always busy.

After midday the men return from the paddock for lunch. Mum had cold roast meat and vegetables with some of her special sauces that I have to learn to make. Then there is fresh bread with jam and cream for desserts. After lunch we all have a rest until one thirty when the day becomes busy once again.

As the men go back to their paddock work, we girls take care of the dishes.

About half past two, Esther and I head out to the paddock and bring in the cows for their afternoon milking. The men arrive back from the paddock just as the cows arrive in the yard. We do the same again as we did this morning. But I take a turn at milking one of the quieter cows and soon get my hand into milking again. It takes me a lot longer than the others but the cow didn't seem to mind at all. If I can get to milk a couple of cows each day, I'll soon have the strength back in my hands again. All that time housekeeping for Pop and Mummy Gomm has made my hands soft and now I need to build the muscle again so I can do my bit. The old Singer sewing machine that works by a treadle that belonged to Mummy Gomm has been left at our home by Pop for me to use when I am mending or making clothes. It is just so much faster than all of that hand stitching. It is such a blessing.

 The dairy work is finished by five o'clock and the men head out to the paddock once again to finish their days work. The girls, Mum and I do some housework and prepare the evening meal. They return back again just on dark and as soon as they wash up, dinner is ready and on the table for them. My goodness they do work hard.

Chapter 10

The work continues just like this all week.
Saturdays and Sundays are the exception.

On Saturdays after the breakfast, the tennis shoes
are whitened and the lines on the tennis court are
remarked with lime and tennis is played by
everyone. The two boys are very competitive and
there is frequent banter about some of the umpire's
decisions. I play a game or two with Esther but she
is more suited to playing against the boys as she is
very nimble and fast on the court and sometimes
she even beats the boys.

The tennis court was made from old termite's nests
which the boys carted in from all over the farm.
They crushed them and spread the compound all
over the levelled ground and with a heavy hand
pulled roller and some water, made a tennis court.
The next thing they will do is build a tall fence with
some chicken wire they have purchased for that
purpose. In the mean time we have to chase those
errant balls all over the paddock and from under
the house.

Some evenings during the summer, they also take
part in some of the local competitions. Serpentine
and North Dandalup both have good numbers of

members and Lance, Clem and Esther take part in
several of their competitions. Clem seems to do the
best in these. Clem and Baden Tonkin from
Keysbrook attended Country Week in the city
competition one year and worked their way into
the finals.

On Sundays, after milking has completed and
breakfast is out of the way, we make sure the time
until the afternoon milking begins again, we make
the day for the Lord.

Dad had been a lay preacher before they left South
Australia back in nineteen twenty six and he still
continues. If there are no convenient services for
them to attend, he holds a church service in the
home and many from the surrounding farms and
home attend as well. Now the Keysbrook Hall is
used for this purpose on some occassions.

During this time the Morrell family move into
Pinjarra. The two sons Jim and Denzel form part of
the church with Jim being sent there as part of the
missionary service. They are such a wonderful
group of people and we certainly enjoy there
companionship and fellowship after the church
services. Eventually Denzel began his own farm
and Jim stayed with the church. Our friendship

with Jim was to last for so many years. He was a bit of a larrikin, with him and Clem always getting into a little mischief. They certainly were two of the same pod, so to speak.

On Wednesday evenings we would attend the North Dandalup Young Peoples Group. Here we enjoyed our fellowship with more people from the local district. Sometimes Jim would visit from Pinjarra too and after our Bible study we would enjoy some little games. In April of 1937, I was elected to join the committee of the North Dandalup Young Peoples Group and my job was to act as treasurer.

Chapter 11

Pop Gomm arrived at the farm on a busy afternoon and we made up a bed for him on the verandah close to Clem's bed.

After talking with Pop, Dad suggested that between the milkings for the next week or so, Lance and Clem could help Pop with the building of our house when he needed them.

Lance and I are so excited that the building of our own house is to begin.

Next morning after breakfast, Lance and I walk over to the chosen site beside the creek, where Pop has laid out the pegs and lines to show where he is to begin building. The initial house would have two rooms with a front and back verandah. He plans to add more rooms to the house as needed and funds become available for the materials.

Pop shows Lance where he needs the holes for the stumps and Lance digs these with his usual gusto. Before we break for a cuppa, he has all thirty of the holes ready for Pop to install the stumps and these are ready for the floor framework before lunch.

Pop's next job is to cut the lengths of timber and fit them to the stumps. I am able to hold one end of these as he drives home the nails.

Next morning Lance, Clem and I help Pop nail down the floorboards onto the framework he completed yesterday. The next job is to make the frames for the walls and Pop has these completed by the end of milking and the first frame is stood up into position.

By the end of the week Pop has the house framing completed and after he attaches the weatherboards to the outside, he fits the corrugated iron to the framework of the roof.

On the back verandah is the kitchen and the dining area. The front verandah which faces the west, has canvas roll up awnings fitted so that they could block out the sun and heat in the summer. After sunset we would roll up the awnings to allow the breeze to cool the house. This also made an ideal sleep-out for Pop for the warmer months of the year.

The inside of our new house is lined with smooth sheeting and Enid, Esther and I apply the light cream paint to the walls. The ceiling is painted white and the weatherboards are left in their natural wood colour.

The wash-house is just six poles and a roof with the copper built into the back corner and the concrete wash troughs mounted on the back wall. There was not enough money left for wall cladding so we limed some old hessian chaff bags and hung these from the roof frame to block out the wind and rain. Lance had Pop build a small single-hole toilet, well out the back and we soon had a path to it from the back door.

After three weeks of building work, we were able to move in.

We did have a bit of pomp and ceremony as Lance carried me over the threshold for the first time. We were so very excited and both felt so very fortunate to be able to live in our own house. We have decided to call out new home the "Wee Hoose", as this is how Pop always seemed to refer to it. I think those words must have come from his Scottish ancestry.

Not before too long we move some more of our furniture in and we settle down to living in our new house. I feel so blessed to be able to have a house to share with my husband and very soon, with a few special touches, it becomes our home.

Life was very difficult during the depression years. Only just enough income for the farm to allow us to purchase just the essential items. I had been living a very frugal life with father and then Pop Gomm and so far that hasn't changed.

We were able to buy some sugar and flour and salt, with the rest of what we needed coming from the farm or our own little garden. We didn't go hungry but we certainly were not able to over-indulge either.

Petrol was very scarce but we did have an allowance for the farm and on the odd occasion we used some of this for driving the little Austin car to church or some other special event. But other than that it was usually the horse and sulky that took us on our visits away from the farm.

My sister Myrtle was confined to the hospital in Katanning just a day before the birth of her first child in June 1937. She and Len named him James Leonard. She stayed there for a week after the birth as recommended by her doctor. They would return to the family farm upon leaving the hospital.

Just two months later, Molly delivered her first child, Laurence, to the world. She and Jim were living in Bassendean and we did get to see them from time to time.

There must be something in the air because I found that I was carrying a child later that year. I was uncomfortable for some of the time but until the last few weeks I was still very active on the farm, doing what was necessary to help keep things working. I has stopped all of the heavier work like lifting and carrying and was doing just the more menial jobs, like bringing in the cows for milking, feeding the calves twice a day and help with the sorting of the fruit. I had several visits to the doctor at Pinjarra, and a few days before I was due, Lance drove me to the hospital in the little Austin car. The road had been sealed all the way to Pinjarra by this time so the drive wasn't as rough as it had been in the past.

Early in the morning of the 5th of April 1938, I delivered my first child into the world. She was a bonny little girl with lots of dark hair. We named her Gwendoline Alice. My sister Dorothy named one of her twins Gwendoline and we both liked that name. Both our mothers had the name of Alice, so that was important to us to use that family name as well. We felt it would do well to help tie the two families together. She was a wonderful child who slept much of the time. Her hair was thick and black, just like mine. Her complexion was of the darker shade, again just like mine but she had a birth mark to the left side of her face. I found this a bit disconcerting for a while but the doctors assured me that it would fade over time.

For the first several weeks after arriving home, I wasn't to do any work at all except for some light house duties. Esther, Enid and Mum were wonderful in helping me get settled in to life with a new family member. Mum was able to give me some advice as she had born four children of her own. In some of my spare time before I gave birth I was able to crochet some booties and clothes for little Gwen and these do come in very handy. We received many gifts from several of the locals who gathered around to help when I came home.

It was so lovely to know that we live in such a community where everyone cares for everyone else. It was the Christian thing for everyone to do and it was so much appreciated. Pop had made a small cot for Gwen to sleep in and she soon grew into it.

With Esther and Enid doing the washing for me every day and Mum bringing us our dinner made it very easy for us to settle into our family life. Possibly because we now have a child, Lance was elected to the position of vice president of the

Keysbrook Parents and Citizen's association. The group always seems to be busy with activities for the local school children during and after school. Of course this would have to fit in with farm work and farm life.

Jim Morrell, the missionary pastor from Pinjarra, spends much of his time working with the young people around the districts in which he works. We usually meet him when we get the chance to attend the church service in Pinjarra and one of the groups he has set up is in North Dandalup which is just eight miles away from the farm. The North Dandalup Young People's Group is still so busy with its functions and Bible studies.

The group still gets together once a month on a Wednesday evening. We participate in prayers and these are always followed by some sort of activity to amuse ourselves. When Jim and Clem get together there will always be laughter as they are both practical jokers and the fun and frivolity is doubled when they join forces.

Like with all groups there needs to be some organisation. Jim is the chairman and the members elect committee members to manage the finances and other activities. I had been attending this area with Pop Gomm several times before Lance and I were married and in the recent past with Lance. At one of the meetings one of the seats on the committee was vacant and I was elected again as treasurer.

One of the activities which we put together was a mock wedding as a celebration of the eighth year of the group, a bit like a birthday party. It was just so much fun to be with a group of similar minded Christian people to relieve ourselves from daily life that can be stressful from time to time, particularly when money was so scarce.

Enid, Lance's sister and Mrs G Hastie set up the tables. Lance's mother made the two tiered cake which had the eight candles around the edge. The evening was to represent a wedding breakfast and this idea was enthusiastically proposed by Enid.

Mr Stan Chamberlain was dressed as the bride, and was known as Miss Eat-a-lot. The groom was Clem and his title was Mr. Saucy Say-Little. Gwen Thorn and I were the bridesmaids while Doug Chamberlain and Harry Johnson were the best man and groomsman. John Button was the minister and he was Pastor Dry-as-Dust. The bride's parents were Mr and Mrs Eat-a-lot and these parts were played by Ron Limb and Lance's sister Esther. Lance played the part of the groom's very best friend, Ted Ramsay, and gave an enlightening speech on his youthful activities.

We had such a great time at events like this and it allowed us to escape the normal events of everyday life.

Another event which comes to mind is a debate which we held. The topic was "Is increased immigration warranted?" This event although of a serious topic turned out to be very entertaining.

In October 1938 the younger of my two brothers, Donald, became married to Vesper, while he was working in New South Wales. He brought his new bride to the property he was purchasing in Gidgegannup. They had six children over the years but one of the girls died at a very early age.

A very large gathering of local people attended the funeral of Mr. A.J. Robinson. It was one of the largest funerals to be held at the Serpentine cemetery. He and his family had relocated from Victoria many years ago and set up farming just to the south of Keysbrook. Mr. Robinson played many large parts in our community as well as his Justice of the Peace duties. His eldest son, Les, continued with the farm, which was known as "Prestonia" At one time Les became ill and spent some time in hospital just after he had cut a lot of hay with his team of horses and binder which lay on the ground in sheaves. His young family wasn't of age to help very much, so a group of us went to his farm after the afternoon's milking and with the help of a few of other locals, we stooked up his hay for him. We got the job finished just before midnight on a bright moonlit night. Les arrived home after being driven from the Perth hospital and arrived just after we had completed the job. He was apprehensive if he would be able to save his paddock of hay but as the car he was passenger in swung around the front gate he got a glimpse of what he called "houses of straw", right over the paddock. He had his wife to drive slowly past the paddock so he could see everything. It's no need to mention that he was extremely pleased to have been able to save his crop of hay but also very appreciative of the help which the neighbours had given him. Such was the attitude of the locals. If someone is in need, we all hop in to help wherever we can.

Chapter 12

The job of milking became more intense as the size of the dairy herd increased. It now has become time to employ some staff to help with the dairy work. One of the earliest employees was Stan Chamberlain who lived close by. He was followed by a number of others as they didn't seem to be able to work as well as Lance and Clem required. On one of the nearby farming properties which the family had purchased was a house. It was used to house farm workers but was just too far away from the dairy, so with the help of Pop, it was shifted. It was relocated just behind the main house and Pop made a grand job of setting it up and added a few rooms to it as well. Esther and I hopped in and gave the rooms a lick of paint just to make it feel more homely for the farm staff who were going to live in it.

Within a few weeks of each other, my sisters, Chrissy and Myrtle delivered babies into this world. Both were boys who would grow up to work with their fathers and work the land together. With the farm requiring so much of our time, so we can have an income, you would think, maybe that we would not have the spare time for outside activities. Well that was certainly not the case. Sundays were always filled with our Christian activities at church or with people attending a church service which Dad held in his own home. We get to meet so many new friends and have such a wonderful time serving our Lord.

Dad is very happy that I am able to be part of the farming team. He has been able to slow down a little and leave some of the jobs which he used to do to the rest of us. Because of the varieties in our orchard, the fruit work is constant. We are always picking, sorting and packing. Some of the unsaleable fruit of course ends up in our preserves. To make my working days easier, Enid and Mum took turns at looking after little Gwen during the daytime.

The Young Peoples Group at North Dandalup occupied some of our spare time during the week and we did so look forward to these activities on Wednesday evenings after the milking had been completed. Esther has been elected to the position of Vice President of the group and I was elected back to the committee again after a break while Gwen was a baby.

Lance, Clem and Dad have become very concerned with the events which seem to be developing in Europe over the earlier months in 1939. The depression which we are experiencing at the time has made everything so difficult. Money is tight and we have a lot of trouble getting the loans necessary to expand the farm. If the difficulties turn into another war, things may get even worse for us. Saturday morning during the summer months, would see us attend tennis events. Esther and both Clem and Lance were very efficient at tennis but I seemed to lack enough confidence and co-ordination to be anywhere near as good as them. Clem and one of our local lads, Baden Tonkin took part in a state event and did very well for themselves.

Towards the end of 1939 my elder brother, Ray, became married to Margaret Shaw.

On the third of September 1939, Mr Robert Menzies, our prime minister, declares war on Germany. It has become necessary for our country to stand beside England and help to fight the advancement of the Nazi war machine. So far they have devastated several countries and destroyed the lives of so many people.

How this situation will affect our lives and farming operation is yet to be determined but we all have reservations and strong concerns.

Hand milking continued until during 1940, when a milking machine was purchased. It was installed into the old dairy much to the consternation of the milk board. It was decided to use the old dairy but a replacement was planned for some time in the future.

I heard many years later that Stan had implored the milking machine salesman not to sell Mr Kentish a milking machine, "because with hand milking it's the only time that we get to sit down on the job." Hand milking allowed us to sit on the little three legged stools while we milked the cows.

I did smile when I heard this as he was quite right, it was the only time we got to sit down on the job, we were all so very busy trying to make the farm business work.

We were producing "whole milk" and for this we were allowed a quota to supply a given amount of milk to the Perth market. This arrangement allowed us to milk all year round and gave us an advantage over the return we received for our milk. It wasn't a lot but enough to make a bit of difference. We continued to produce "whole milk" until the 1970's. To support our dining table, I had Pop and Lance make me a vegetable garden behind our home. With cow manure and straw from the dairy we were able to produce a range of vegetables for our home and also for the main house. Carrots, cabbages, lettuce, cucumbers, grapes, onions, radishes and strawberries were my main crops which I could attend to after the days farm work was finished. My strawberries were producing very well one season but presently the production dropped and I could not see the reason why. Pop came to me one evening and told me that he had spotted little Gwen helping herself. She was picking them straight from the bush and eating the delights without me knowing. I scolded her and said that she must not touch the strawberries as they were for all of us to enjoy. So the production of the increased for a time but then dropped off again. I just happened to look out the kitchen window one morning and there was Gwen, down on hands and knees eating the berries right off the plant. When I scolded her about this she replied "but Mum, I wasn't touching the strawberries".

The Church services which Dad was holding in the home had become very popular, even with some of the folk from the city. A group of Salvation Army lads and lasses drove out to the farm to take part in the services. Many would stay on for a cuppa or for lunch which was available for them. Esther received a letter in the mail from one of the lads. It seems that Allan Uren was very interested in her friendship.

Allan was living in Maylands where his parents had a small shop. Allan had Salvation Army connections and would attend Church with them for the fellowship. They became engage and had yet to set a date for their wedding.

In May 1940 another of my nephews arrived. Myrtle gave birth to Colin Victor in Katanning hospital and was soon back at their family farm. With the participation of Australia in the war in Europe, there has been a call to arms. The Australian Army is looking for recruits to strengthen its forces. Allan and many of his Salvation Army group have joined 2/16 Infantry Battalion as Army bandsmen. They were to be heading out to the front sometime later in the year.

Dad had a deep discussion with Esther and suggested that they should become married prior to Allan going away to war. Even as a bandsman he would be facing danger. He felt it would be easier for Esther, should Allan not return, to go through life as a married woman rather than a spinster. Dad's sister, Alice had lost her fiancé during World War one and she had a very hard time and Dad could not let this happen to Esther. This had a further advantage. In as much as Esther was able to see much more of Allan prior to his going away than had they not married. They took his advice and set the wedding date for the eighth of June 1940.

Their wedding ceremony was held in the Anglican Church on the south bank of the Serpentine River near the road bridge. The very reverend Ron Limb, who was stationed at Pinjarra at the time, and Mr Doley, from the ministry of Booleroo Whim *(In South Australia where they lived before Keysbrook but now living at North Dandalup),* jointly officiated at the ceremony. Allan's brother, Cooper, was best man and Enid was bridesmaid with little Gwen traipsing along as flower girl. Esther wore a lovely white wedding gown which had been specially made for her. Dad was very emotional (a common family trait) and just before the parade down the aisle, Esther needed to settle him down to control his nerves. Usually it's the other way around. Esther along with the rest of us had been teaching Sunday School at Serpentine each Sunday. The children provided a lovely "guard of honour" for the bride and groom outside the church after the ceremony.

A grand reception was held at the home on Bolinda Vale. Enid, Mum and I had set up the back verandah for the occasion with what decorations we could muster up and set out the refreshments for everyone who attended. After the dinner had finished Esther and Allan spent their honeymoon at Kalamunda with £10/0/0 to cover the cost.

Allan went away to Army camp at Northam a week after the wedding and Esther returned to the farm. She was able to visit him in Northam on several occasion. Usually she would take the train from the Keysbrook station and travel to Perth, Here she would change trains and head to the east. The Army had its own station by the Northam army camp, so her travel was sorted out.

Allan and his unit was shipped out in October 1940 and by Christmas he was in Palestine. He saw no action here but was doing a lot of training and some sightseeing. Allan did a lot of writing home and Esther has kept the letters of this era. They would be very interesting reading!

The 2/16 Infantry Battalion was shipped out from the Middle East and taken to the fronts in New Guinea. As they travelled via Java and Fremantle, Esther was able to spend some brief time with Allan while the ship refuelled in Fremantle.

Allan spent much of his time tending the wounded until he himself was injured by the Japanese. Esther received a telegram from the Army to say that he had been wounded in action and to express their deepest sympathy. The telegram arrived at the Keysbrook Post Office which was run by Mrs Bee. She handed the telegram to Clem who was there to collect the mail and he gave it to Esther at home. Several days later a letter arrived from Allan in which he explained what had happened and that his injuries occurred to his hand and arm by a rifle bullet. He was confined in New Guinea and later transferred to a Hospital in Queensland.

We needed another car and Lance was able to buy a used Austin 10 with a fabric roof. Quite a good little car and a bit bigger then the older Austin 7. As the trains were reserved for troop transport in 1942, Esther travelled to Sydney on board the ship "Katoomba" to visit Allan in hospital. He was later discharged from the army in 1943 as he had returned to Perth and was working for Mr Bell at his chicken hatchery. Together they built themselves a home in Bayswater and visited the farm frequently but with the petrol rationing it was difficult.

Molly and Jim had a second son arrive when she attended Fremantle hospital. Barry was born on 14th September 1940. She was home again a week or so later. Laurence stayed with us on the farm until we visited her a week after she returned home from hospital.

We arrived home on the train just in time to attend the funeral of Mrs Scarf. Lance was one of the pall bearers at the funeral ceremony at the Serpentine cemetery. Reverends Ron Limb and C Doley conducted the service. Mrs Scarf had two sons and a daughter who would sadly miss their mother. The community would sadly miss her too as she was so busy in the district helping others, sometimes to her own detriment.

Our family is growing again. Chrissie has just delivered a daughter, Audrey Christine on October 13th 1940. She would join her brothers at home on the farm shortly after.

During World War Two there was a substantial Army Camp just to the northeast of Mundijong, George Marriott and Roy Lane were two of those troops who were stationed there for a time. Les Gomm, the son of Pop Gomm, was the Padre at this Mundijong Army Camp. So with this affiliation through the Gomm's, some of the soldiers would be taken to the farm for visits and Fellowship. One of these frequent visits was a "singsong" night on Wednesdays. George formed a lasting friendship with us and we enjoyed many reciprocal visits over the years only ending with his death in 1990. Les Gomm went on to become the Minister in the Adelaide Baptist Church in the 1960's.

Fred Burt was the son of the Methodist minister from Pinjarra, who was having health problems and came to stay at Bolinda Vale for some time. He survived on a diet of oranges and he maintains that this is what corrected his medical problem. He went on to become a Church of England Minister. As fate would have it, he was Padre for the 2/16 Infantry Battalion and met up with Allan again whilst in Palestine.

Soon after War was declared both Lance and Clem
attempted to join the Armed forces. Clem tried on
several occasions to join the R.A.A.F. but his
application was rejected each time on the basis that
he was involved in "essentials services" (that of
providing materials and foodstuffs for the war
effort and the population). Lance too, filed several
applications to join the Armed Forces but each of
these were also rejected for the same reason. So due
to the Manpower Act they were deemed to be of
more benefit to the Country to stay on the land and
provide this service. Dad was getting on in years
and not very well and if the boys were not there to
work on the farm, it would have gotten into
disrepair or even disposed of. Although
disappointed at not being able to be part of the "big
action", Lance and Clem accepted the situation and
continued with the farm.

Reliable farm staff was a problem to find prior to
the war years but now with many men going away,
this problem was much worse. This caused
everyone on the farm to work even harder and
longer hours or even trim their activities to work
around the staff that was available. Holidays were
curtailed during this period and with some
mechanisation they were able to cope with the
situation. With male staff being so difficult to

obtain, we needed to attract female staff to help work the orchard, dairy and farm. The advertisements in the newspapers were as long as my arm as all farmers were in the same situation. We had several women working on the farm from time to time and Alice Hitch was one of these. She was a lovely young lady who fitted in with the family well and liked to look after Gwen when she was able. I was expecting my second child soon and I needed to curtail the heavier of my work as I was becoming tired more quickly. Mum said that this was probably just the fact that I was carrying the baby and not some other problem. I was fit and healthy so that would make such a difference. Some farm machinery was available now, so Clem and Lance got hold of a hay baler that was driven from the belt pulley of the tractor. This was a stationary unit and the hay needed to be carted to the baler. The material was forked into the chamber and the plunger would compress it. When the bale was long enough a board was put in to separate it from the next bale and they tied off the string by hand. Now they could make about 300 bales per day. This now made the handling of hay much quicker and more convenient. The stacking was a breeze with these rectangular bales. There was still a fair amount of manual work involved but this new hay baler was a forerunner to increased farm mechanisation.

My father spent a few days in Katanning Hospital in April 1940, after he suffered a few minor injuries when his car crashed. He was badly shaken up but his wife was there to look after him. I was heavily pregnant and did not feel the travel to visit would be wise.

Our second daughter, Marjory Ruth, was born in Pinjarra Hospital on 26th of April 1941. Soon after our return to the farm, Pop Gomm added a few rooms to the north side of the "Wee Hoose" where he would make his home. One of these rooms had a seat built in under a window. As years went by, the girls were often found playing in and around it. I had nursed Pop's wife during her last days and he found this way to repay me for my efforts. He was a great friend to all and helped the family in the home and around the farm, thus either alleviating some of my workload or allowing me more time to help around the farm.

Little Marjory was a handful and she looked into everything just as soon as she could crawl. We needed to keep a close watch on her as she was soon able to move around very quickly.

Father was back in Katanning Hospital again in July. It seems that perhaps his car accident may have caused him more harm than first thought. Father was working as a labourer for one of the local farmers and he was poisoning rabbits which had become such a problem. It seems he may have suffered a stroke while working. He passed away on July 24th 1941.

Our growing family, with Lance and I, along with Gwen at three years old and little Marjory just three months old attended the funeral. We drove down in the little Austin and stayed with Dorothy and Harrold on the Hillside property. It was a very sad day but also a great time as we were able to catch up with my brothers and sisters with their partners and some of the little ones who we had not seen before.

Just a month or so later Myrtle gave birth to her first daughter. Kaye Lynette was born on 12st September 1941. They are living at Inglewood for a while now while Len is away with the army.

Chapter 13

Mum was carrying a bag of fruit to the wagon which was pulled by the old horse in the orchard when she got her foot hitched up in a tree root. She fell over with the bag of fruit landing on top of her, I was working close by and heard her yell out. After checking to see that she was safe she complained about it being hard to breathe. I ran to fetch Lance and Clem to help and we managed to get her into the little Austin car and I drove her to the hospital in Pinjarra. The doctor confirmed that she had a cracked rib and should stay in the hospital for a few days just to make sure there were no other injuries. She remained there for three days and could not stay another minute as there was nothing for her to do here. I returned in the little Austin and took her home again. She was so pleased to be back in familiar surroundings and carefully do some of the lighter duties that we would allow her to do.

Dad was an old man. He had worked extremely hard and for many long hours over his lifetime. He had seen many changes in society, properties, farming, and family. The Church and family were the things which he held dearest to him and these were with him even after the end of his life.

Edward Joel Kentish passed from this life on a

quiet sunny afternoon at home, Bolinda Vale, on June the 26th 1942 at the age of 75 years and 3 months.

In his Will, he bequeathed the property of Bolinda Vale and adjoining properties to his wife Edith. She could foresee problems with this arrangement and after a family discussion, decided to divide the property into equal shares for her 4 children. The property was professionally valued and divided. While all agreed that this would probably be a better arrangement, Lance and Clem could also envisage further problems. As that arrangement stood, they would be working hard long hours, developing the land to improve its production and the girls would benefit from this by way of an improved asset for no input. While they did not wish to be selfish they were not happy to do this. Lance and Clem raised sufficient capital, paid out the two girls their share of the property, thus allowing them to work the land and build up their property while giving the girls the capital to carry on their own lives. This arrangement between Lance and Clem was the beginning of "Kentish Brothers ".

Enid was teaching music at Pinjarra and occasionally on her return journey, she would be met by a young chap driving a Ford truck fitted with a gas producer. Enid would accompany him and spend some time at his poultry sheds and a "cuppa" in the incubator room. Reginald Robert Courtney Ingpen was his name and he often came to Bolinda Vale to visit Enid and play music. Reg was a very gifted musician having learned, as a lad, the flute. He was adept at playing the piano and violin much to the delight of Enid, her mother and everyone at Bolinda Vale. Reg earned his living operating his poultry farm and selling the skins of the rabbits he had trapped in the hills.

Radio was in its infancy at this time and Reg was very adept at making and repairing radio apparatus. He had made several "Crystal Sets" that he would listen to each night. Reg and Enid corresponded by letter frequently and Enid was taken by the nature of the man who wrote these letters. Reg proposed to Enid and on July 28, 1943, they become engaged.

Esther delivered her first child, Beverley Joy on 23rd of March 1943. When she arrived home after her confinement in the hospital she had a complete change. Now she could not spend so much time helping Allan with is activities and was needed to spend more time in the home caring for her little one. It must have been a big change because she was always so busy on their block of land in Bayswater.

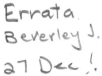

Errata.
Beverley J.
27 Dec !.

On July 20, 1943, a large gathering, met at Bolinda Vale, the occasion being in connection with the Glen Forest Christian Endeavourers' and friends Reunion. Mr. Les Gomm, who was the president of the Christian Endeavour movement for some time, was the speaker. He has recently been padre to the Mundijong soldiers' camp and was able to attend. Several of the group came from Coolup, Pinjarra, and many from North Dandalup, where we go to attend the North Dandalup Young Peoples group. The meeting was very impressive and uplifting. We helped Mum provide supper which seemed to be enjoyed by everyone.

Margaret had her wedding on 21st August 1943 when she became married to John Lyle Lambie. He is of Scottish heritage. Margaret had been staying with Molly for a few weeks just before the wedding which was held in the Methodist Church in Claremont.

It must have been the year for weddings as Connie and Ralph Lowe had their wedding on 8th December 1943. She had joined the armed forces and trained as a nurse. She was posted to the hospital at Northam and later at Hollywood hospital. Ralph, also in the forces was a lieutenant. After a brief honeymoon, they returned to their own barracks. They intended to live in Melbourne when the war was over.

131

Gwen began her schooling when she attended Keysbrook State School in 1944. There was daylight saving during the war years and School didn't start until 10.00 a.m., much to the dismay of the locals and parents. Marjory was just two and a half so I was able to leave her with Mum while I took Gwen in the little Austin to her first days. After that she had enough confidence to ride her horse. With Lance being vice president of the Parents and Citizens Association, he organised a busy bee and stables with yards were built beside the school, so all of the attending students and their teacher could leave their horses in the yards during school time. There was unusually five or six horses in there during school hours.

Most farm children helped around the farm when they weren't attending school and with daylight saving there weren't enough daylight hours when the children returned home from school in the afternoon but it allowed them more time in the mornings. Gwen was able to assist me around the house and help with little Marjory when she wasn't at school.

Chrissie gave birth to her second daughter in October 1940, Lynette Margaret was born on 9th of March.

I was expecting my third child and was not very comfortable. Constant tummy niggles were causing me a lot of concern. After talking things over with mum, she suggested that I have Lance take me to the hospital just in case this little one wanted to arrive early. The doctor said that the baby shouldn't be here until the middle of July but it seemed things were not quite right. The doctor checked me out and I stayed in the hospital overnight and then he sent me home again as he said everything was all right and that I had two weeks to go.

Well, I was back in a week or so as my labour pains had begun in earnest. My third daughter, Lorna Joyce came into this world on the 12th of July 1944. The doctor was unable to explain to me what had caused the problems but they all disappeared now that I was holding my little girl in my arms. Such a delightful little one with dark hair and a dark complexion, very much like mine.

While I was confined to Pinjarra Hospital, my sister Molly came to stay at the "Wee Hoose" to look after Lance, Gwen, and Marjory while I remained in the hospital with Lorna. She brought with her Barry and Laurie, her two sons who were about the same ages as Gwen and Marjory. When Molly called them for lunch one day she could not get any response, so she continued calling. Still getting no response for some time she began to get worried and started looking for them. She eventually found them up to their knees in pig muck in the pig sty. She took them home and washed them down with the garden hose before she could put them into the bathtub to get then clean. Even after a good scrub they still smelled of the pig sty for several days. Margaret delivered her first child just on their first wedding anniversary. They named him David Muir Hamilton Lambie.

Enid and Reg's courtship continued to flourish and they became married on November the fourth, 1944. The ceremony was held at St. Steven's' Anglican Church on the south bank of Serpentine River. Yes, the same church that Esther and Allan had used. Enid wore a long white frock with a veil borrowed from Mary Lunn. Esther and Dorothy Day, who were dressed in blue frocks attended Enid while our youngsters, Gwen, and little Marjory were the pink dressed flower girls. The reception was held in the Serpentine hall with Mrs. Perrett and Mrs. Manning supplying and arranging the flowers. Mum made her famous yeast buns and Mrs. Pennell made and decorated the wedding cake. After the reception, Reg and Enid retired to Allan and Esther's home in Bayswater. Among their wedding gifts were petrol ration tickets (*due to wartime restrictions*) and clothing tickets.

They made their first home on "Hilcot" where they lived until their house was built on "Ellora". Enid and Reg spent some memorable time planning the house and surrounding buildings. The house which cost £52/10/0 to build was constructed by Mr. Philips. Harry Fawcett built the chimneys for £25/0/0.

Clem decided at an early age that he would participate in local government affairs and was elected to the Serpentine-Jarrahdale Roads Board in 1944. He was Chairman for 1944-1945. He held a position in local government for many years and was recognised for his efforts later in the 1990's.

A property about one mile to the north along the Bunbury Road came on the market and after inspecting it, both Lance and Clem agreed that it would be a good purchase. They bought this property, known as "Mount View" from Mr. Wells. When they took possession of it they cleared away all of the rubbish lying around and found a lot of useful (to someone) implements and farm items and tools. They held a clearing sale to dispose of the unwanted gear and deposited a fair amount of money to their loan account. The sheep which were on the property were sent off to the abattoir as some were showing signs of footrot. The old Mount View homestead was situated near the railway line down Fisher Road. This house was used for staff accommodation for many years. Near this house was a set of sheep yards and a shearing shed complete with a well and windmill. Between the house and the railway line, there was an old orchard and closer to the house were some large grapevines. These were Muskats and a cutting from here was taken and planted at the new house when it was built.

The old shed that they had been using for milking the cows on Bolinda Vale was in need of extensive repair and becoming too small. Rather than spend time and money fixing it they decided to upgrade and build a new dairy.

To construct the new dairy they used gravel and sand which came from the creek, mixed with cement to form the concrete which was used for the floors and walls of the dairy. All materials were loaded onto the horse-drawn dray by hand using shovels and then mixed by hand on site. They were able to employ some local men to help with the construction. Pop Gomm was the overseer of the building, Mr. Harry Fawcett (from Scarp Rd.), Mr. Maurie Fisher (from across the railway line) were some of those who assisted in this work. After the concrete floor was laid, timber plank formwork was erected to form the concrete walls. When the cement set, the planks were removed and used again and again. Timber trusses were fitted on top of the walls and corrugated asbestos roofing material fitted. The Mac Donald milking machine was installed and this was one of the newest and most modern dairies in Western Australia.

Soon after the new dairy had been constructed, Lance and Clem were looking for an alternate supply of water. Mr. Westcott who had a property west of Keysbrook had some success at divining for water and suggested the most likely place to dig, just happened to be in front of the dairy. The young men armed themselves with a pick, shovel, windlass, and bucket then began digging. They continued with this very difficult and dangerous work until they reached about 60 feet. Although they encountered a patch of water washed stones they didn't find any water. Mr. Westcott couldn't understand this so he pitched in to help with the job. They reached 75 feet and only a trickle of water on top of a hard base so they had to stop at that. A very frustrating result for all of the hard work that went into the job. However, they put a windmill to work and used all of the water which the well would produce. But they continued to rely on water which was drawn from the creek which is known as Dirk Brook.

Marjory was only a toddler at the time when she had a large doll. She was playing around near the dairy and stables and the well that had not long been completed. She was getting upset with the doll because it would not talk to her. Eventually she had had enough of no response from the doll so she walked over to the well and threw it down. When she realised what she had done, she got upset and then the tears started to flow. Someone saw the situation and went down the well and recovered the doll. Although it was wet and soiled Marjory cuddled the doll and the tears went away. I don't think the doll would speak to her now even if it could.

Chapter 14

Their father had been a tremendous guiding influence to Clem and Lance but many of his farming ideas were outdated. After his passing they were able to operate the farm in the manner which they considered to be the best way. They made many decisions regarding the methods of operating the farm and of carrying on the business, all of which have proved to be successful. We had begun our family so Clem and Lance decided that they would work their way to building up a farm that could easily be divided to make two separate units. This would give each of them a farm in their own right that each could operate with our own families. This proved to be very good forethought but was many years before it eventuated.

Now that the farm was providing a steady income from the production of Whole Milk, Lance and Clem were able to extend themselves and purchase more land around the farm. Much of this land was bush or fairly roughly cleared so they were still working hard to develop this and bring it into production.

The dairy herd was increasing in size and performance as their land holding increased and property improved.

Mr. Gobby had a property that he had purchased from Mr. Mathews which adjoined Bolinda Vale to the south. He was running sheep and during the good seasons did very well out of them. However, he could not understand what was wrong with his sheep at one time so he called on Clem to determine the cause of the problem. The sheep were flyblown and when Mr. Gobby saw the damage to the sheep and the agony that they were in, decided that he didn't want anything more to do with sheep and decided to accept Lance and Clems' offer of purchase. This was 160 acres and being only divided by a fence line was an ideal addition the farm.

Vermin are always a problem with farming and during the 1940's there was a plague of rabbits. Lance and Clem mixed some "1080" poison grain baits and laid them out around the paddocks and in the next few weeks the dead rabbits would be picked up. Quite often our little Gwen would be driving the horse, Lilly, and cart while the two men walked alongside and threw these dead rabbits onto the cart. They would do a few loads each day between milkings, so that would represent about 2 tons of dead rabbits daily. The dead rabbits were thrown onto a heap of timber and the set alight. The stench of their burning bodies was very strong.

Lance has not been able to eat a rabbit stew since.
We take the train into the city to visit Molly several
times. She is expecting her fourth child in the early
months of 1944 and for some time has been having
a few different experiences to her previous
pregnancies. The reason for this became evident on
the fourth of April when she gave birth to twin
boys. Both she and they were very healthy. It is not
unknown for a twin to bear twins but it seems to
run in our family. Max and Ross are identical twins
except for those who know them well.

Just a few weeks later Esther delivered her second
child, Lyle. He had difficulties at birth but with a
good effort the doctor was able to allow her to
leave the hospital with him a few weeks later on.
Apparently he suffered a lack of sufficient oxygen
while he was being born and this has caused him
some difficulties which continue for the rest of his
life.

Gwen has a new teacher at Keysbrook. Miss C
Davies is accommodated at the main house where
Mum looks after her wellbeing. The school now has
several classes with about twelve pupils and she is
able to control and teach them all without too much
fuss. At least that is what we are led to believe. She
rides her push bike alongside Gwen on her horse to
and from school most days.

I could ride a horse, drive a horse and buggy, drive a car, drive a tractor or truck but I was not able to get my balance to enable me to ride a bicycle. In later years I did buy a push bike with two wheels at the back. This I was able to ride but that's a long way along in my story.

The war years passed on so very slowly. We know there were hardships where our brave young men and women were fighting for the freedom of the world but we had many hardships too. The government was wanting us to produce more milk with less inputs. The price we could get for our fruit and milk was just enough to cover our costs and give us a week's holiday each year. We had a number of women working in the dairy and on the farm but still we worked from before sunrise to after sunset with just a few short breaks during the day. We were so very tired.

Connie was working as a nurse until she was a few weeks from delivering her first child. Glenys was born in the middle of September of 1945.

Enid, too, was expecting her first child. She seemed to have difficulties for most of her pregnancy but in November 1945 she gave birth to little Roger. He was a sickly little boy. It was just so sad when he passed away when he was just five days old. Enid and Reg were so very broken hearted. The rest of us really felt for them but rejoiced in the fact that our children were healthy. We spent some very quiet days around the houses and farm in that period of time.

In the middle of 1946, Esther delivered her second son, Graeme in this world. He was a chubby little chap and always smiling.

A few months after little Graeme arrived we read of a report in the West Australian newspaper about how Lances cousin the Reverend Rupert Kentish aged 39 of Darwin had been executed by the Japanese during the war. We knew he was missing for several years, assumed to be killed but now the details are laid bare in the newspaper report. It was another dastardly deed carried out by the enemy during that time, but this one is so close to the family.

My sister, Margaret delivered her son Lyle towards the end of 1946. Such a chubby little chap who loves to be fed.

Another of the events which keep our little community together is the annual Christmas-Tree event which we put on for the little ones each year just before Christmas. We spend some time decorating the Keysbrook Hall with whatever we can get hold of. Ivan Elliott dresses up his old horse drawn buggy, complete with bells and drives this from the railway station to the hall. The children are so happy to have hay rides on the horse drawn buggy. Most of them do it on the farms at home but this is an evening affair, just on dark. Once the rides are completed everyone assembles in the hall and gather around the decorated Christmas tree and receive gifts which are handed out by Mr Elliott posing as Father Christmas. Following this there are many games which have been organised for the children to play and by the end of the evening we drag them away to their beds. It is such a lovely time when we can all come together and enjoy our time with each other.

A new teacher arrives at Keysbrook. Miss E Stewart takes over the education of her pupils. She is with us for about a year.

Just into the New Year of 1947, Kerry arrives. She is the new daughter of Connie and Ralph. A sister for Glenys.

Marjory begins her first year at school. She rides on the same horse as Gwen has her sitting in front of her on the horses back. Sometimes she uses a saddle, but usually they go bare back on the old horse.

A few months later and Enid is confined to Pinjarra hospital where she gives birth to Joan. Enid is so pleased as there are no difficulties with the delivery and this baby survives.

Our Harvest Festival is another event which brings our community together.

This is also another of our Christian celebrations. Once again the Keysbrook Hall is decorated and everyone brings along something which they have produced on their farms. There are many eggs, chooks, lambs, calves, colts, sheaves of hay, butts of grain, vegetables of all varieties, butter, cream, milk and cheese. Sometimes it can get a bit rowdy as the young animals begin their talking while Lance delivers his sermon.

Lance is elected to the position of vice president of the Keysbrook School, parents and citizens group. One of the community suggested that they take the children to visit the airport at Guildford. The stock crate was fitted to the old Ford truck and about twenty children accompanied by their parents climbed aboard. The trip to the Guildford airport was comfortable for those of us in the cabin but no one on the back complained. Once at the airport everyone jumped down from the open truck and we all visited the airport buildings. Here we were able to watch as several large planes landed and their passengers walked down the stairs, across the tarmac and into the building. At the same time another plane was being loaded with its passengers. They too, walked across the tarmac, climbed the stairs and into the plane. A few minutes later we could hear the engines start up, then the plane began moving along the taxiway and eventually the runway. The noise increases as the plane picks up speed and soon it points its nose to the sky and leaves the ground behind. Lance's cousin, Keith Nicholls is a pilot with one of the airlines and he has just come in from a flight. He explains how everything happens on board the plane. It was a very informative night and most of the young ones really enjoyed themselves. The journey home was quiet on the back as many of them slept.

Around the middle of 1947, three young people come to live and work on the farm. Roy, Ken and Margaret Marsden made their way down from Geraldton and moved into the newish cottage which we had prepared earlier. Both Roy and Ken were good hands in the dairy and being fit and healthy, both worked in the paddock alongside Clem and Lance. Margaret helped me in the house with Lorna who was just three years old and a handful. Lorna has not learnt to crawl yet but bounces along the floor on her bottom. Such an unusual method to get around but she seems to enjoy it.

Lance has a special name for her. Bouncer.

The education department is shifting our teachers around again. Miss E Stewart who stayed with Mum and Clem in the old house is leaving to go to Capel and Mrs Mumford arrives to take her place. Sunday School is still being held in the Keysbrook Hall. Pop, Lance and I take the classes each Sunday and show the little ones the teachings of our Lord in a manner in which they can understand.

Lance, the girls and I meet up with Evelyn Stewart as we take a little time to holiday in Busselton. We can only be away for a week, so we make the most of our time at the beach and campfire cooking in the evening. Sitting around the campfire at night and sing songs and hymns. We put the cattle crate on the back of the old Ford truck and we sleep under a tarpaulin stretched over the top of the frame.

We get home just in time to hear from Esther who is soon in labour with her second daughter. Lynette is born around the middle of January.

The new school year is interrupted as Marjory is taken sick. We didn't know what was wrong. She complained about chest pains, her heart was beating rapidly and she was very tired all the time.

Eventually the nosebleeds made me take her to the doctor who was visiting in Serpentine. Dr. Whelan had a look at her for a few minutes then said that I should take her to the hospital in Pinjarra as he thinks that she probably had rheumatic fever. She needs to spend 5 weeks in hospital and after recovering at home for a few more weeks, she returns to school. We have some pushbikes for the girls now but Marjory isn't able to ride hers. She has half days at school for a month or so, before she returned full time. Margaret has been such a big help during her illness.

The Parents and Citizens of the Keysbrook School are helping the children to work in their school garden. To the local heavy clay is added manure, sand and wood ash to provide a better growing environment.

I am with child again, expecting in January. After three daughters, Lance and I are hoping for a son. He would be able to help on the farm once he has grown some. The pregnancy is different from the first three so here's hoping.

In August my sister, Margaret delivered her daughter, Isobelle. And just a week or so later Enid produced a son. Edward John. She was so terribly worried after the events of her first son but was very relieved when Edward was so much healthier. He was named after her father.

Chapter 15

Labour pains began for me later in January. Lance drove me to the hospital in Pinjarra just a few days before our first son was born. We named him after Lance's grandfather, David Joel. He was a bonny child with a shock of very dark hair and a similar complexion to myself. We left hospital a week later and returned home to a great welcome. Margaret had the house in good order. It seems she and the girls work together very well with the washing, cleaning and cooking.

Pop Gomm was there to welcome us too and that was a real pleasure. He had spent a few weeks with his daughter, Clarice at their home in Manjimup.

Just after the middle of the year, many of the women of the district joined together at Enid's home for a meeting with the Rev. Brayn of Pinjarra. The object of the meeting was to form the group known as the Keysbrook Ladies Guild. We would meet at different homes once a month for prayer, Bible studies and to swap recipes and so on. It was a lovely few hours that we put in between our other activities. Little David stayed at home with his sisters in Margaret's very capable care. I arrived home just in time to feed him.

Lorna begins her first year at school. It was very hard to leave her at the school on her first day or two. But she didn't seem to mind the school work as Marjory there to help her with any difficulties. Gwen had completed her education last year when she finished her seventh year at school.

The events of the Keysbrook Ladies guild continued on for quite a number of years and often in our home too. We covered many aspects of conversation and had different clergy attend to lead us in prayer and deliver some sermons which many kept us laughing for days. There was always a cup of tea and cake afterwards and I certainly enjoyed the companionship of the other ladies. Lance and Clem purchase a block of land across the railway line from the Mount View block. This 160 acres will provide some more grazing land for the dairy cows. Being a bit further away from the dairy this is usually where the dry cows and young heifers are paddocked. In April of 1950 the Ladies of Keysbrook held the inaugural meeting of the local branch of the Country Women's Association or the CWA. After a few years some of the men in the district referred to us as the "Chin Wagger's Association". The CWA in Australia was booming as there seemed to be a need for women of the districts to assemble and share. There is a bit of the "women's guild" here too and after several years it folded as we recognised that the CWA could deliver the same compassion and companionship as the guild did. Unfortunately neither mum nor I was able to attend that particular meeting as we were needed in Perth for another event. But we joined at the next opportunity to be part of the group. We had a lot of fun, learning new skills and discussing different events. Sewing skills improved for some many of the ladies and as the younger ones joined in they too began to learn these skills.

Flower arranging was one of the topics that we covered and when we were able to, we held our first CWA Flower show in the Keysbrook Hall during October in 1950. It was a grand event for our first effort with several ladies visiting us from other CWA groups. These events are always concluded with a cup of tea and a cake or two. The fellowship that we all enjoyed really made a difference to our daily lives as we were all so very busy with our farms, families and general living. Enid joined the group after a few months and she was still helping the guild to continue.

Just a few weeks after our first CWA Flower Show one of the more prominent ladies of the district passed away. Mrs Bessie Bee who had been our local Post Mistress for many years and formation member of our CWA. Her funeral was held in the cemetery at Serpentine. Lance was one of the pall bearers and I made up a very fitting wreath for the occasion.

The Keysbrook Hall seems to be busy now it is nearing completion. The last of the windows has been installed to close off the cold wind and allow some natural light to enter, particularly during the daytime.

The Scaffe families are leaving the districts to live nearer the coast. They developed a property along the Bunbury

Road just to the south of Keysbrook and had sold this property to Mr. Jack Money who had more property at North Dandalup. We held a big send off for them at the Hall. So many people attended. The Scaffe's and Bassett-Scaffe's had been involved in so many of our activities in this small district. They had been involved in the local P and C, CWA, Farmers Union, Methodist Church, Keysbrook Ladies Guild and the Hall committee just to name a few.

A week after the Scaffe's send off, my sister Margaret delivered another daughter. Carol was born on the 28th of October. I really don't think that the small family which left England all those years ago to find a new home in a new land would have expected the size of the family to grow as it has. They experienced such tough times and so many happy times and so many sad times over the years, it makes me wonder what Mother and Father would think if they could see us now.

Into the new year of 1951 saw another new teacher at the little single room school at Keysbrook. Mr Brian McGinity started at the school at the beginning of the year. This was Lorna's second year so now she could help with the younger ones too. The next year he and his wife moved in to a house on Hectors block which we purchased.

Little David was having difficulties with his left ear. He was having trouble hearing and there was a reddening of the flesh near his left ear. Dr.Whelan suggested that he may have a middle ear condition known as mastoiditis and that he would need to spend some time in Pinjarra hospital where they could drain the fluid. He was home again after a fortnight with a scar behind his left ear to show where the operation had taken place.

In the middle of 1951 I was pregnant again, this time with my fifth child. I was having quite a few difficulties and Lance suggested that I take some time off and drive down to visit Dorothy during the school holidays. That seemed to be the only time she was home with her family due to her teaching duties. It was a lovely drive down and I called in at Pop's daughter Clarice in Manjimup on the way. Morning sickness was my main problem and she gave me some ginger beer that made a big difference. Dorothy allowed me to sleep in but I found this very difficult as I'm used to be up before sunrise. But I was able to relax some while I was with her and we caught up on all of the family news which I had been missing out on. It was such a lovely time to spend at Dorothy's but like all good things, it came to an end. The little Austin car took me home again and it was so good to get home again after that week away.

Gwen has fitted into the farm work very well, she is just so good with the calves and horses. She seems to be able to have them do things that none of the others could. Perhaps it has something to do with the fact that she spends a bit more time with them. She is up with her dad every morning and brings in the cows for milking.

She is in charge of the separator so that we can have some cream for our table. After daylight she feeds the calves with some milk and hay and makes sure they are well housed and so on.

It is approaching my time for confinement so Alan and Lorna Dick, (Lorna is Lance's cousin) take Marjory and David to Dorothy's so she can care for them while I spend the time in hospital. Pop takes Lorna to be with Clarissa, his grand-daughter, in Manjimup. Margaret is able to take care of the house while keeping house for Lance and Gwen.

My time in hospital was difficult and sleep was a problem because of back pain but on the 18th of November I delivered our second son, Neil James. In spite of the problems which I had experienced, he was fit and healthy and had such a loud cry when he was hungry. He had Lance's complexion and hair colour and was always very active.

Just a month or so later, Enid was in hospital, this time to deliver her second son, Robert. Such a chubby little chap and Enid was happy with her family of three.

All of our houses seem to be filling up, so Pop added a room to our "Wee Hoose" by the creek and Reg added a room to their home to accommodate the extras in their family.

The farming operation is continuing to prosper. Another bush block has been purchased which keeps the men busy between milkings.

Lance keeps a tight control of all the dairy feed. They had a stack of bagged bran in the feed room and for some reason he happened to see a man helping himself. The man verbally abused Lance and sped off in his car with the bran in the boot. The police were called and they eventually caught up with the man near Cannington. Lance was required to appear in court where the man was convicted of the theft and he had to pay all of the court costs too. It turned out to be a very expensive bag of bran for him.

The men decide that the 200 acre block of land that is for sale by the Hector family to the west of the other block they bought a few years ago would be a good buy. It joins the other block and gives them more pasture for the cows.

After the evening milkings, Clem would take off in his Vauxhall and visit a young lady in Subiaco. He got some ribbing from a few of his local mates about always being away from home in the evenings but eventually he became engaged to Ira, the daughter of Dr Eric Smith. She had attended Perth Technical School where she had trained as an artist. They became married in the Wesley Church in the city. Clem's tennis mate, Baden Tonkin was the best man and Ira was attended by her sister Valma. It was such a lovely affair and they drove to Geraldton for their honeymoon.

Very soon after they returned to the farm and made their home in the old house, it was decided that they should have the house to themselves. With the help of Pop Gomm and Mr Bob Stillwell they build a flat for Mum to live in beside Esther and Alan's home in Bayswater. At the completion of this they continued with some renovations to the old home to update it and make it more liveable for the young couple.

Esther was very happy with this arrangement as now she could be just a few steps from her mother instead of an hour's drive.

Soon after the work on the old house was completed Pop Gomm took some time for himself and drove his old Chev van to Manjimup to spend Christmas with his granddaughter.

Between Christmas and New Year, Esther delivered her third daughter, Shirley. Allan spent some time to enclose one of their verandahs to make more sleeping room for their increasing family.

In 1953 a large block of land a few miles to the west of Keysbrook came on the market. Lance and Clem could see the value of the improvement to their farm if they bought this land, so they arranged to purchase it from the vendors. It was low-lying and largely uncleared with several swamps included. It was three square miles in size and needed to be fenced, so that took them many weeks of work to cut the trees, split the posts, dig the postholes, install the posts, run the wires and make a boundary fence. Many weekends would see us take the children, pack a picnic lunch and work on the block between milkings. Quite often friends would be with us too.

Ira and Clem are the proud parents of Coralie, their first born who arrived in July 1953. Ira had a difficult time during her term but was happy now that she had her daughter.

Horses were still being used on the farm for many jobs and Gwen and Marjory can relate memories of them. Most of these were Clydesdales. Bonnie, Jimmy and Lilly were draught horses. Blossom died in the early 1950's after she got into the wheat for the chooks. She ate too much, became bloated and died. The girls were very upset one morning when they looked out into the paddock and saw the old horse laying there all bloated up with her four legs sticking straight out.

The girls were a big help around the farm between schooling. Quite often during fruit picking season you could see them with a horse harnessed to a cart, standing on the side of it picking the fruit from the trees. If Lilly was being used she occasionally would just gently move forward, grasp an orange in her mouth, squeeze it to break the skin and swallow the juice. Then spit out the skin. Jimmy and Bonny were not so gentle and occasionally caused a few problems. With so many varieties of fruit trees in our orchard, there was always picking, sorting, packing and marketing the fruit. A fruit grader was bought to help us with this job and that made so much difference to the amount of work that we had to do.

The Keysbrook CWA continues on with fortnightly meetings in the Keysbrook Hall. At one time someone came up with the idea of trying to knit with matchsticks. With very fine thread this was possible but so many of us had trouble keeping the thread on the matches. It did create a lot of fun and laughter and it was enjoyed by all who attended. Our annual Flower Show is held in October and I won a few prizes with some of my annuals.

Since the war had finished there seems to be an increase of the disease, Poliomyelitis. It caused so many trouble in so many people. We came to meet one of the sufferers of Polio and became friendly with him. Cliff Tomlinson was also a character. He got on well with Clem who was also a bit of a jokester. He had lost the use of his legs as the muscle had withered away. Quite often he would chase the children around the house by folding his legs in front of him and scooting across the floor on hands and bottom. He could move surprisingly fast. Cliff visited us on the farm frequently and also stayed with Esther in Bayswater too. He was careful with his hands and made models of aircraft and boats. Cliff had a motorised wheel chair and this allowed him to be more self-sufficient. It was such a sight to see him driving his wheel chair down the road with David on his push-bike alongside him on the way to Serpentine.

14th November 1953 is Serpentine Show Day. We attended during the morning and stayed for lunch but had to return home for the afternoon's milking much to the distress of the children who were having such a good time. Neil was walking now but we did take the pram in case he became tired and needed his sleep. I had some jams and preserves in the show but didn't get any prizes. The girls were more interested in watching the horses in the centre of the showgrounds doing their jumps and so on.

Chapter 16

After the war years, good dairy staff was still a problem. Working with the Department of Immigration, Lance and Clem were able to successfully sponsor a family to work in the dairy. The Marsden's had moved out of the house so we had work for them as well as accommodation. The Heerema family arrived and had settled in by the beginning of 1954. Case and his son Claas would work on the farm and dairy while the three daughters attended school or helped their mother in the house. They could speak only broken English so sometimes there was a language problem. They also had a son Jacob who was blind. Apparently they had worked on a dairy farm back in Holland and found our methods and farming so much different.

Pop Gomm has moved to be near his daughter in Manjimup now and although we still keep in contact, we don't get to see him so much now.

In July David is having considerable difficulty breathing with a lot of wheezing noise coming from his chest. I take him in to see Dr Whelan in his Serpentine surgery and he suggests that he has asthma. This contracts the bronchial tubes in his lungs and makes it very hard to breathe. He has some pills to take a couple of times a day and if it gets any worse we should take him to the hospital in Pinjarra.

In the evenings we have the fire in the lounge room stoked up to provide some warm dry air for him and this seems to help him a lot. We all enjoy sitting by the fire on the cool or chilly winter nights, it is just so comfortable with the children around. I sit by the fire with the light on so that I can keep up with my knitting or crocheting, the boys are playing with their meccano set on the floor but we all stop when Lance begins telling his stories. He has a grand imagination and makes up little stories that include the children. One of his favourites is the magic carpet stories. He keeps us all involved and enthralled with his telling of them. In later years he tells these same stories to our grand-children. He just changes the names around to suit his audience.

Marjory attends Armadale High School for her first year in 1954 and was required to ride her pushbike to Serpentine to get onto the Armadale School bus driven by Mr. Bill Fitzgerald. She was leaving home about 7:00 in the mornings and returned home about 5:00 in the afternoon. It made a very long day and added to the difficulty of study.

At the office bearer's elections for the CWA, I was elected to the position of vice president while Gwen became the treasurer.

Mum turns seventy seven this year, so we bring her down from Esther's to spend some time with us at the "Wee Hoose" as our home had become known. She is showing her age but still enjoys being with the family and spending time at the farm where she has spent so much of her life.

Esther, Alan and their family were not able to attend as Esther was in hospital giving birth to Glenda Bell. Her second name comes from an ancestral surname of several generations ago of the Nicholls family which was Mum's family.

Several times over the years I drive the girls up to Araluen to visit the tulips when they are flowering. It is such a pretty sight and good to see the delight on the girls faces as they can take in the beauty of the place. The bush setting with the big arbours do set off the picture of the area. Sometimes Lance and the boys come too and we have a picnic on the lawn. We get such joy from seeing this display of God's work. I try to get to the Perth Flower show as often as possible as they have some gorgeous blooms there too. But getting away from our busy lives can sometimes be difficult.

While Clem is busy with the local roads board, Lance has spent quite some time with the Farmers Union. This takes him away from home several times each month as he attends meetings and visiting politicians for the betterment of dairy farmers in Western Australia. In July 1954 he is elected to the position of second vice president in the whole milk section of the Farmers Union.

There are many changes to the way we do things on the farm and there are more changes on the way. Lance holds several meetings with other whole milk dairy farmers around the local districts and presides over meetings to discuss the start of bulk milk handling. Our ten gallon cans have done a good job but bulk handling seems to be the way of the future.

Lance became ill and was admitted to St. John of Gods Hospital in Subiaco for some time. Gwen was only 16 or so and had to operate the hay baler for that season. Marjory and her friend, Diane O'Leary, went to visit him. They dressed in their smartest clothes, put on lipstick and a flower in their lapels. When Lance saw them with their make up on he gave her such a dressing down as he considered her far too young to be painted up like that.

Close to the edge of the Bunbury Road, just inside the paddock was a giant Morton Bay fig tree. This tree covered a large area and was an ideal place for a cubby. Our children spent quite some time playing under this tree. One of the games was to tie a string around a block of wood wrapped in brown paper to make it look like a parcel. This was then placed in the middle of the road. When a motorist stopped to pick it up the kids would pull the string and the motorist thought that the parcel had disappeared. We used to put the address of 60 Wyatt Rd, Bayswater on the package but don't think any got delivered. That was the address of Esther, Alan and their family.

The kids were very fond of Mills and Wares ginger nut biscuits, which we purchased by the large tin. They often had a few in their pockets. Neil lifted up one of the old bags that covered the floor of the cubby under the tree and found some worms. He liked playing with the worms so he put some in his pocket. Later when we returned home someone asked if he had a biscuit in his pocket and when he put his hand in, he pulled out a mess of biscuit and worms. From this day on he had the nick name of "Grub".

Pop Gomm made a small box type cart fitted with a pair of lightweight shafts and bicycle wheels. This was fixed to a pet billy goat with a harness and the kids would have rides and a lot of fun. Sometimes an old pet sheep named Buster would be harnessed to the cart.

At the end of the 1954 school year at Keysbrook, we hold a send-off party for Brian McGinity and his family. He has been the solitary teacher for all of the children who attended the school for the last few years. The Government has seen fit to close the school as numbers do not warrant it being open any more. The children will have to attend Serpentine or North Dandalup state schools in the future.

The Parents and Citizens Association in Serpentine has lobbied for a school bus to collect children from around the district to deliver them to school and return them home again in the afternoon. Mr Bill Fitzgerald has the contract for the bus and he employs Mr Ted MacMillan from Serpentine to drive it for him. Lorna and David are able to hop on the bus by the front gate, so they are spared the bike ride. But because the bus is a bit late arriving in Serpentine for Marjory, she still needs to ride to Serpentine to catch the bus to Armadale high School. This is David's first year at school.

Clem and Lance were proceeding with their plans to operate the two separate farms and Lance took the opportunity to call tenders for the construction of their new home. Mr. Bob Stidwell was a young budding architect from Gosnells and was retained to draw up the plans for the brick and tile dwelling.

After locating the site for our new home I had some input for the design. Because we looked out towards the hills I wanted a large widow so that we could see out. Our old home only had small windows and I was happy when Lance agreed with me. Lance had wanted a passage that would also double as a breezeway to cool the house with the sea breeze which happened most summer days. We needed three decent sized bedrooms so that we had our room, the three girls shared their room and the two boys had a room for themselves. The front verandah looked out towards the Bunbury Road and the hill while the back verandah looked out over the paddock.

Lance selected Plants of Waroona as the building contractors as he had seen some of their work previously and was happy with it. The house was

completed for habitation in June 1955 and was fitted
with all the "mod cons" such as 32 volt power and a
toilet built onto the back verandah. No more long walks
to the outback dunny.

A small shed was constructed to house a diesel engine,
generator and a set of batteries. We had them fit in some
large cupboards into the dining area so I could house
my preserves and materials for dressmaking.

A well had been constructed some years ago with a big
windmill fitted to it. This supplied water to the house
and for the stock. There was a lot of "coffee rock" in the
well and this caused the water to stain everything an
orange-brown colour. This made the water unsuitable
for the house so a large concrete water tank was
constructed to hold the rainwater as it came off the roof.

Clem and Ira are the proud parents of their first son.
Colin is born to them after Ira had spent a couple of
weeks in confinement and a week in hospital. Her good
friend Mrs Knobs, looks after her household while she is
away.

David's asthma is bad this year and he is in Pinjarra
hospital for a week so they can help him. It is so
terrifying to see him suffer as he tries to breathe. Soon
they have some different medication for him and he
returns home.

I have been elected to Vice President of the Keysbrook
CWA again with Gwen still as treasurer. She seems to
do a good job of this. I baked a cake which Gwen iced

for the CWA birthday party which we held in the old hall. Discussions soon begin about the future of the old school building. We work out that if we could buy the building for 50 pounds, providing the land was for free. This was accepted by the education board and we held our first meeting in our new club rooms in April the following year.

In October of 1956 we get the news from the Reverend Les Gomm of South Australia that his father, our Pop Gomm had passed away. We knew he was getting on and had a few health problems recently but we didn't expect him to pass at this stage. I had begun with him caring for his wife, such a long time ago. We spent so many happy hours together and he had done so much for us in return. It was a bitter pill to swallow but he had lived a full life and helped so many people and children over his life with the spreading the word of God everywhere he went. He did so enjoy taking Sunday School and seeing the delight on the children's faces when he told them of the stories of Jesus.

Gwen has developed into a strong tennis player. She attends tennis in Serpentine at every opportunity. She and Lance often have a hit on the old tennis court in front of the old house.

Lance and I had both being providing Sunday School lessons at Serpentine for many years and Lance was made Superintendent (His father had held this position in South Australia). While Mr. Laurie Manning took the

Sunday School at Serpentine, Lance and I would travel to Mundijong and hold Sunday School in their local Church. Lance was also quite busy with Lay Preaching and would frequent Jarrahdale, Pinjarra, Waroona, Mandurah and Byford churches.

Neil began his education in 1957 when he attended Serpentine State School with Lorna and David. The following year Lorna would commence her secondary education when she attended Armadale High where Marjory had just completed her secondary education. Marjory had finished high school in 1956 and started work on Bolinda Vale in January 1957. She and Gwen worked together with their father and uncle until Gwen left just prior to her wedding. One of Marjory's favourite jobs was to get the cows in for milking. She would saddle up the horse, usually Sandy and sometimes Trixi, and ride around behind the cows and drive them to the dairy. On one wet day she decided to keep herself dry and wore a raincoat. Unfortunately it flapped in the breeze and this startled the horse, Sandy, and he bolted across the paddock with Marjory clinging onto the back of him. She tried to fold the coat tails under her bum to sit on them but every time the horse moved, she lifted off the saddle and the coat tails came loose again. This frightened the horse a bit more and off he would go faster again and the faster he went the more noise the coat tails made. After 15 or 20 minutes she was able to get him under control and then by removing the raincoat she was able to walk him back to the dairy. A scary experience to say the least.

The local Junior Farmers hold their gatherings in the Mundijong Hall. Gwen attends here whenever possible and this is usually during the evenings. They seem to have a lot of fun and fellowship while discussing some of the various farming practices and other activities within the district. Many of the young men and young ladies from around the district attend and Gwen usually had a ride with some of them. It is at one of these events that she met a young man that she was attracted to. His family had a mixed farm at the back of Byford and they soon became friendly.

Our first born is engaged to be married. At Just 19, Gwen is to marry her sweetheart, Fred Swaby in June 1957. The event will take place in the Byford Presbyterian Church with the reception to be held in the Byford Hall. For months Gwen has been collecting the wishbones of chickens which have ended up on our dinner table. She covers many of these in foil as part of the decorations for the reception tables. Every one attending can make their own wish as they break the wishbones.

Many of the ladies from our CWA also help her with the collection of decorations that will be used for the event, too.

We are moving stock along the Bunbury Road near the Mount View farm and Lorna is struck by a car. Luckily it was only travelling slowly and she received only a bruised hip, but she had a noticeable limp when she assisted Gwen at the wedding.

The wedding went off very well with Lance walking proudly beside our daughter as they walked down the aisle to meet the groom and his group. After some photos were taken we moved to the hall as it began raining. The ladies have done a marvellous job of the decorations. Streamers, flowers, ferns and so on filled the stands around the sides of the hall. The tables were all set out with white table cloths and vases of flowers and wild oats wrapped in coloured foil in the centre of the tables. Each place setting its own silver wishbone. Many of the well-wishers are from the Junior Farmers, the tennis club and of course the families. After a short Honeymoon, they moved into a house on one of the Swaby properties, west of Byford.

Esther successfully delivers her forth daughter, Merle into this world. Their little house in Bayswater is near bursting at the seams but they are a tight Christian family and they all work well together.

Our little CWA rest room is progressing very well and now we have quite a library of books. Some are new, some are a bit older but are well presented now that I had the chance to assemble and sort them out using the author's' names. Most have been donated by our local ladies and some were left behind by the old school. Some renovation is required to make our rest rooms just that little bit more comfortable. We ladies do the painting after the builder has completed his part.

About eleven months after their marriage, Gwen delivers her first child. Our first grandchild. Audrey Lynette is a bonny little girl with mop of dark hair. The week in hospital is like a holiday for poor Gwen as she gets to do most of the work around their farm. She is strong and capable and able to set her hand to any task that she has at hand. Not long after they return home from the hospital a new house is designed and the building begins.

At our November meeting of the CWA I once again am elected to the position of president. I gain so much pleasure from working with these ladies and sharing our fellowship time together.

Ira has missed a few of our CWA meetings as she has a little difficulty with her pregnancy. But it all works out well in the end when she delivers their second daughter, Heather.

While we were living at the old farm, Lance walked from our home to the dairy but now he drives the mile over to the old farm for milking and farm work. David and Neil had an experience that would have far reaching effects on their future. Lance took them with him when he drove over to Bolinda Vale to help with the milking one day. He put David and Neil in the boot of the Austin A40 car. The reason for this is not clear. When Lance arrived at the dairy he had his mind on other things and left the car and went directly to do the milking, inadvertently leaving the boys in the boot of his car. The boys thought that he was having a game and would be back soon but after some time they became agitated. However hard they kicked and banged on the boot lid they could not make themselves heard and they became very upset and distressed at being locked in such a confined space. It wasn't until the noisy milking machine was turned off after the completion of milking (about two and a half hours) that someone who was walking past the car heard the noise and told Lance. He exclaimed "Oh my goodness the boys are in the boot, I completely forgot them". He immediately unlocked the boot and out came two very upset and frightened young boys. To this day both David and Neil have extreme difficulty in containing themselves in a small enclosed area. The experience has left them with a feeling of strong claustrophobia.

Both Lance and Clem had property in the hills and this was becoming increasingly difficult to fertilise by hand. The other option was to use aeroplanes for the purpose. These were expensive but still the most cost effective way to do the job. At the end of Fisher Road in Fletcher's paddock was the first air strip as the old Tiger Moths required a fair distance to get enough height to clear the hills. This strip was used for several years and at one time they used a small strip just over the creek from Mount View homestead across the Bunbury Road from

Karnup Farm. When the boys returned home from school on the bus one day they saw this aeroplane tail poking up in the air with the nose of the plane resting on the ground and told me as they ran in the door. Apparently a gust of wind had caught the plane as it was preparing to load up. It was blown across the strip and through a fence. During the 1960's, Clem and Lance along with some other locals constructed an air strip up in the hills near Scarp Road. This made the operation much faster as the planes were already on top of the hill when they loaded up. Clover seed was added to the super prior to spreading and now there is a good body of clover through the hills blocks, providing good stock feed.

Chapter 17

In 1959 Marjory was to begin her Nursing career. She had worked fairly hard on the farm and was happy for the change. Marjory studied at Fremantle Hospital whilst living at the nurse's quarters and was home frequently on the weekends and for some of her holidays. She studied and worked at several hospitals in W.A.

Lance and I took a driving holiday to Tasmania in January 1959. We put our car on the train that went from Perth to Adelaide. The two nights on the train were marvellous and we met some nice people who were travelling east as well. After driving our Austin A90 off the train in Adelaide we drive it to Melbourne, we put the car on the boat and departed for Tasmania. We spent 3 weeks there and had a good rest and looked at some dairies as well. Mr. Joslyn was one of the people whom we stayed with while we were there. As we left home we were experiencing a heat wave and this followed us for all the time that we were in Tasmania. Lance had a new Ricoh 35mm camera and was adept at taking some great photos of our trips. Unfortunately the smoke haze from the fires made it very difficult for him to get the best photos. We drove to so many places down the east coast then through Hobart. Here we stopped for a few days and looked in on the Botanic Gardens where they had a magnificent display of begonias. Then we drove up to Launceston where we stayed for a few days before heading west to Wynyard. Tasmania is such a lovely place with its rolling green hills and then there are the mountains to the west that we could see as we drove along. Some of the waterfalls that we visited were magnificent too.

The drive home from Victoria to Adelaide seemed so much quicker than the drive east but we were happy to be on the train again on our way home. When we arrived we find everything in good order. Mrs Boyer had stayed in the house and she looked after everyone very well.

Upon our return we began designing a new dairy.

I always had lovely long black hair that was usually plaited and tied around my head. David and I were trying to get a temperamental lawn mower to go. David was pulling on the rope starter and I tried to help him. Unfortunately, probably due to lack of experience, I gripped the belt and pulled too but when it rotated around the pulley it pulled my fingers in as well and severely damaged two fingers on my hand. My goodness that hurt. I was taken to hospital for attention but the fingers were strapped up for a few months. Because of the discomfort of the damaged fingers I was not able to do my hair and after having Lance and the girls do it for me for some time, decided to get it cut off to a style that I could manage. Now it just needs brushing and it falls into place.

Esther delivered their third son in November 1959. Kevin Ross was to always be the baby of the family. During 1959 we began the construction of the new dairy in preparation for the forthcoming dissolving of Kentish Bros. and subsequent splitting up of the dairy herd. We selected the most modern design that we had seen when visiting the various dairies during our recent trip to Tasmania. The design allowed for the cows to step up onto the milking level while the operators worked at the lower floor level. This made milking a lot easier on the back.

The dairy was constructed by Green and Saw Bros. from Armadale and the welding fabrication was completed by Barry Jubb of Jarrahdale. A lot of care was taken to make sure that the floor slopes were correct and the drainage was adequate. With a further elevation of the milk room, the job of lifting full cans onto the truck was much easier. A diesel engine was used to provide power for the vacuum pump and also for the 32 volt generator. An overhead line was put in to connect the 32 volt system of the dairy to that of the house to make life a little easier. Eventually the engine and generator at the house was dismantled and the shed was used to store our firewood.

Lorna completed her education at Armadale High in November 1959 and immediately began work on the farm with Lance and Clem. She fitted in well with the

dairy and stock work doing those jobs which had
previously been done by Gwen and later, Marjory.
Lance was becoming increasingly concerned with the
less fortunate youth around Perth. He was on the Board
of Directors for the Mofflyn Children's Home in Victoria
Park with the Methodist Church. They set up a farm at
Werribee (near Wundowie) where boys who had come
through the court system would be given housing and
care whilst they were instructed in farming activities
and practices. This also involved some farm work which
was very beneficial to them as they would be better
absorbed into the community with some new skills.
However there are some people around who did not
agree that these boys should be made to work, albeit for
their own benefit. When the boys were no longer
permitted to work, others needed to be employed thus
causing the operating costs to increase. The Werribee
operation had to be closed down and the farm sold. The
boys who were there were so sad to miss that
opportunity.
Mum had been showing her age for some time now and
she eventually suffered several strokes. It was too much
of a burden for Esther to care for her anymore, so we
sought out a suitable nursing home for her. Several that
we tried seemed unsuccessful for a number of reasons
but we settled her into an aged care facility in Mount
Henry. We would visit her, usually on Sunday after
church but we could see that although she was being

cared for adequately, she was deteriorating. She passed away on 26 January 1960. Her funeral service was held at the cemetery in Serpentine where she was interned in a grave alongside of Dad. Because she was so respected and busy in the district for such a long time, people came from all over to attend and pay their respects.

The dairy herd continued to grow and in the year just prior to the herd being divided, they were milking 250 cows twice each day. At the time, this was the largest dairy herd in Western Australia and we were producing about 500 gallons per day to fill the whole milk quota contract.

The days that both Clem and Lance were dreading had arrived. This was the time to divide not only the land but also the dairy cows, machinery, tools and other stock. For years they had worked together amicably and now with the dividing up of everything, that period of their lives had come to an end. It was a very stressful time for both men to divide their belongings and go their separate ways but they had planned for this day and knew that it was the correct thing to do. There had been no animosity amongst either of the men or Ira and myself although sometimes things did tend to get a little difficult. Our Christian upbringing had stood by the men and they overcame those little problems in the most Christian manner.

Lance and I formed a partnership and had the paperwork all completed before the split up. We also had our own stock brand and this is described as the letter **J**, followed by a lazy**1** then the letter **V**. so it looked like: $J \mathord{-} V$.

Now that they were working separately each would need to learn to be more proficient in the activity that the other had been better at. Lance learnt a lot more about stock work fairly quickly as did Clem learn more about the mechanical aspects of farming.

We each took about 125 dairy cows along with a quota of about 250 gallons per day. The cows of ours were driven along the road after the mornings milking to their new paddocks. Now the fun was to start. Lorna remembers working on Bolinda Vale after she completed her final year at Armadale High School. She helped sort out the cows and drive them along the road to Mount View. Marjory was home for a weekend from nursing at that time and she helped sort out the problems that they had teaching the cows to step up onto the raised floor in the shed. Marjory, Lorna, Lance, Ted Hoad and I soon had the system worked out and it certainly was a much easier dairy to work in.

Most of the older cows fitted in to the new dairy remarkably well but some of the younger ones didn't like the change and balked at the step. With some careful handling they overcome the problem but production did suffer for some days. But we had plenty of manure.

During this same year, Lance was elected to the position of President of the Whole Milk Section of the Farmers Union of Western Australia. He was prompted to this position by the crazy widespread prosecutions of dairy farmers on the debatable question of milk quality. Lance would attend meetings in Perth and regionally very frequently and held this position for 8 years.

We continued to employ farm staff and we had two houses for them to live in with their families. The Henderson family were working on Mount View in the 1960's with both Ed and Herrick working on the farm. Mrs. Henderson was a very large lady. Lorna had a pet budgie in a cage on the back verandah and had just taught the bird to do the wolf whistle. Mrs. Henderson needed to speak to me and had walked up from the house near the railway line. Just as Mrs. Henderson came through the side gate she was greeted with this perfect wolf whistle. She was not impressed. She was quite flustered from the walk up the paddock and to be greeted like that was just not on. She complained to me about the problem and I apologised for her discomfort but it was difficult to keep a straight face.

Gwen who had been working hard on their farm again was confined to Armadale hospital where she bore their first son Eric. Such a lovely little fellow who spent much of his time sleeping.

The old house on Bolinda Vale was showing signs of its age when Clem and Ira began building a new brick and tile house close by. They designed the house with 3 bedrooms with an office and double garage under the one roof. This new home was a vast improvement on the old home which was then used as a workers cottage and subsequently converted to the Museum.

In February of 1961 there was a major fire in the hills area. For a week, fire fighters battled against the advances of the fire beast but it eventually covered an area from Kingsbury Drive, right near our home to Pinjarra and east for many miles. Things were looking fairly grim in the district and Marjory was called back to the farm from her nursing to assist with the dairy while the men were attending to the fire. The Dwellingup Township was razed completely and several people lost their lives. Lance, Clem and many others spent 15 or 20 hours per day in the attempt to help bring it under control. One night, the fire was approaching the Bunbury Road from the east, so a back burn was started along the highway in front of Mount View just a hundred yards from our front door. As this was burning and encroaching up the hill, the east wind began to blow, causing some burning cow pats to roll along the ground and sparks from them were lighting up fires in the paddocks immediately to the west of the road. A team of men spent all night mopping up these little spot fires and saved any damage to Mount View. Lorna didn't have her driver's license at that time and the local traffic inspector, Mr. Bill Fitzgerald, turned a blind eye when he saw her driving the little Austin truck and water tank. After it was all over the Army arrived and lit their own fire to cook their breakfast. This didn't go down very well with the locals. Marjory was driving the tractor with her father standing on the water cart behind. They were putting out the small fires around the wooden fence posts and on the edge of the back burn. The Army guys began laughing as they had obviously not seen a young sheila driving a tractor before. Gwen came to help as well but had to stay in the house as she was pregnant with Doreen at the time. Fred was out with the other men with his fire unit. So it was all hands on deck when there was a crisis.

Lance organised a hay supply for those people who needed some feed for their stock and a large stack of donated hay was built just east of the dairy. The unfortunate part of this is that some people who were not fire affected also took advantage of the free hay, much to the disgust of Lance.

Our CWA has been going now for ten years so we decided that we should do something a bit different for our celebration. We held the event in our new home and showed a group of slides of our Tasmanian trip. With the Dwellingup fires fresh on everyone's mind there were many comments on the smoke and haze on so many of the colour slides. We had a grand time and finished the event with cakes, scones with fresh cream and fig jam.

Lance's cousin, Keith Nicholls had married Kitty Mortlock. Her family had a Ford dealership in Fremantle. Lance and Keith were talking about new cars and he suggested that we should take some time and visit the Ford assembly plant in North Fremantle, which we did during the school holidays taking the boys with us. It was great to see how the cars all come together on the assembly line. The new model that was released had a wagon in its range and on seeing this we decided that when the time comes we may have one of them. We did have and old Ford 10 years ago and it seemed to be good but we did have such a great run with the range of Austins which we had owned. So in January 1961 we did buy that Falcon wagon, a blue one. It seemed to suit our purposes very well as the boys could sleep in the back when they were tired on our frequent evening's outings.

Doreen Rose is the second daughter born to Gwen and Fred in July 1961. Gwen didn't seem to stay in hospital for very long this time as she wanted to get back home. I had Audrey stay with us and Eric was looked after by Fred's mother.

In 1961 the New Local Government Act was gazetted which changed Road Boards to Shire Councils and Road Board Members, to Councillors. The Chairman was now the President. All Road Board members were to retire and an election was held within the Serpentine-Jarrahdale Shire to elect seven new Councillors. Clem was elected to the position of president, topping the poll. He was to continue either as president of the Shire or a councillor well into the 1980's.

We had been holidaying in Rocking ham for a few years and seen so many people enjoying their boats, so we bought a small bond-wood boat, fitted with an 18 horsepower Johnson outboard motor. We all spent many happy hours at Rockingham and Palm Beach playing with the boat and learning to water ski. This was later updated to a larger boat with a 40 horsepower outboard motor and now they could ski much faster and continued to have fun as a family. This use of the boat was usually done between milkings on the weekend and during the two weeks annual holiday at the beach.

Lance's cousin, Keith Nicholls, his wife Kitt and their two sons Don and Peter were very keen skiers and boat people and we spent many hours with them together enjoying the sport.

An adjoining block of land came on the market and it seemed like the sensible thing to do to increase our holdings. On September 1961 we paid a deposit and agreed to purchase a 74 acre property from Mr. Atkins. This block adjoined "Hectors" and "Fishers" and was referred to as the "New Farm". It was divided into two paddocks and had a well with a windmill on for the stock water.

David attended Pinjarra High School in 1962 and 1963 for his secondary education. By riding his pushbike the 3 miles to the Keysbrook store, he was able to catch the bus to travel the next 15 miles to Pinjarra. Starting out at 7:30 in the morning and returning by the same route in the afternoon, arriving home at about 4:30. Edward Ingpen was at that school at the time

In the early 1960's the Government was involved in a program to provide electric power to the south west of the State. Mr. Arthur Farnham was the electrician who carried out much of the initial installation work in the district and was kept very busy. Most farmers would erect their own poles and he would come along and fit the cross arms and insulators onto them and carry out the necessary wiring and connections.

Lance was honoured by the Judiciary of Western Australia, when in 1963 he was bestowed with the honour of Justice Of The Peace. Among his other responsibilities in this position, he also was deeply involved with the establishment of the Karnet Prison Farm. Along with Clem they sat on the Bench of that Prison for many years.

November of 1961 saw Lorna begin her Mother craft Nursing at N'Gala. She studied nursing and worked at N'Gala until March 12, 1963. Lorna has been attending Junior Farmers along with Gwen and Marjory when she was home from nursing. There are several young men who also attended and she was attracted to one of the

young men in particular. Barry Robins was his name.
He lived in Armadale with his parents and was running
a small orchard on Eleventh Road, down past the drive-
in theatre. When he was not working in his orchard he
was working as a cabinet maker for one of the larger
firms beside the railway line near Queens Park. Lorna
and Barry became engaged in July 1962.

Lorna and Barry married on the 26th of October 1963.
After their honeymoon they settled into their new house
on Eighth Road in Armadale.

I do so enjoy my time with the CWA and I was elected
by our local branch as a delegate to the state conference
to be held in Perth. It was a noisy affair with so many
ladies trying to out talk the other. But the meeting was
well run by the president and we achieved so much.

Close to the end of October 1961, I was proud to make
the best use of my new electric mix-master. I won the
best cake in both the Byford show and the Serpentine
show a week later. There was a lot of competition too
with Gwen also taking out a prize for her preserves in
the Byford show.

Lance engaged one of the men from Serpentine to
enclose our side verandah. This would make a lovely
sleep-out for the boys as theirs seem to be the warmest
bedroom in the house, particularly during the summer.
We moved their double decker bed out there for the
warmer months. The girls also had beds on the side

verandah to so that they could sleep in a cooler part of the house during summer.

The old Austin truck which Lance had bought from Len Green of the Keysbrook store has finally packed up. We knew this was coming and Lance had looked at several options over the last month or so. The Bedford truck seemed to suit our purposes the best, so at Sydney Atkins motors in the city he placed the order and we picked it up on the 17th of February 1962.

We had the State Electrical Commission power connected to our house on June 1st 1962, with Clem and Ira having theirs connected two days later. Until this time they were relying on a 32 Volt DC system. Now both I and Ira needed to purchase those electrical appliances that were necessary for the modern kitchen that we take for granted now. These included a refrigerator, freezer, Lightburn twin tub washing machine, mix master and electric iron. I could add more appliances to this list as time went by. A couple of years later I was able to upgrade the old treadle sewing machine for a new one that runs off the 240 volt power. At Bairds, I was able to buy a Minerva electric sewing machine and it is such a delight to use. I have trouble keeping my feet still.

Power was connected to the dairy in June 1962. This made working in the dairy a little easier as the noise of the diesel engine was replaced with the quietness of an electric motor. There was still the noise of the vacuum pump and the pulsators but this did make the job more bearable. The lights were much brighter as the old 32 Volt lights were fairly dull. Because of frequent breakdowns with the new power supply, the old engines were left in place to operate the dairies when the power went off.

Neil and David have been putting up with some old pushbikes for some time and Lance took the opportunity to buy them some new bikes for Christmas. These came from Glasson's little bike shop in Gosnells. These are very modern with three speeds for them to have fun with.

Our dairy has been supplying both quota and surplus milk to Masters for many years now. The price of our quota whole milk paid us a premium but the milk which was surplus to this amount was paid at a much lower rate. Browne's Dairy have offered us a much better price for as much milk as we can supply them. So for a while we can benefit from the extra income.

The hay season was about to begin for 1962. We had an older hay baler that keeps breaking parts and Lance traded this one in and bought the new International baler from Daly's in Byford ready for the new season.

I stepped down from the position of president of our CWA and Ada Fawcett was elected to this position. I was elected to the position of secretary. Apart from other duties I was able to record the minutes of our meetings and write the letters.

It is two years since we bought the Falcon wagon and it has done us proud. Lance is of the opinion that if we turn our cars over before they begin to give trouble we should be able to have trouble free motoring and the cars will hold their resale vale better. So with this in mind we traded in the wagon and purchased a new Falcon. This time it is a fawn coloured sedan.

Because Lance is now a Justice of the Peace, we are invited to attend the garden party to greet our lovely young Queen and The Prince of Edenborough on their visit to Perth in March 1963. It was a very glamorous affair with so many dignitaries from across the state attending. She walked down amongst the group of us and I curtsied and Lance bowed as required when we were presented to her.

Marjory has been nursing at Beverley Hospital and she has met a handsome young man. Soon they became engaged and it seemed that before very long they were married. This occurred in September 1963, just a month before Lorna and Barry's wedding. The reception was held at a hotel in South Perth with Lance driving our car as the wedding car. While they were driving from the ceremony to the reception through some crowded streets, a little girl ran out from between two parked cars and Lance collided with her. She had a head injury and after Marjory attended to her she was rushed off to hospital in an ambulance. Lance was so very upset but as the policeman had told him, he was not at fault. It did not make much difference, the little girl was injured by his car while he was driving. He was very quiet for the rest of the day which could not finish fast enough for him. We talked about the incident in bed that night and he broke down and cried, he was just so upset.

The next day Marjory and Greg visited the little girl in hospital and she was on the mend. The doctors were satisfied that there would be no permanent disability to her.

Chapter 18

In our travels around the place of our holidays and our recent trip to Tasmania we were taken by the idea of having our own caravan. We looked around at several of the local manufacturers and settled for a Ravan caravan which is built in Subiaco. We bought this caravan late in 1963. It is lovely. Two tone blue on the outside with the inside finished in gloss white. Barry who is the cabinet maker in the family says that the workmanship is of a high standard. It suits our purpose very well and Lance is delighted in the way it just sits behind the car while we are travelling.

David who had completed his second year at Pinjarra High School last year, is off to board at the Narrogin Agricultural School. Lance has been talking to Grant McDonald who is the president of the WA Farmers Union who lives at Toolibin, just east of Narrogin and he recommend it. He is also a patron of the school and knows how the system works. It is a two year course and will give him an insight to other aspects of agriculture as well as some of the more modern techniques. We drive over to Narrogin and leave him behind in the care of the teachers. It is difficult to leave him there and I hold back the tears as we say goodbye.

Marjory and Greg have been living at Lake Grace for some time. He works as a stock agent while Marjory is nursing at the hospital. She had to stop work for a while as she gave birth to their first son, Stephen in March 1964. We drive down with the caravan and spend a few days with them as she is discharged from hospital with her lovely little boy.

The CWA has me busy again and over the next few months we have meetings in our new home, then a CWA Birthday meeting at Esther's place in Bayswater. Dorothy's visit coincided with one of our meetings and she gives a talk on some of her experiences at several of the schools that she used to teach in, some years ago. Joan, Enid's daughter was elected to the position of treasurer towards the end of 1964.

We have several tractors on the farm to do all of the farm work that is necessary. We have used Fordson Farm Majors and Fordson Dexta's for many years and now has come the time when we need to trade in our last Fordson Major. It has done us proud with only a few minor problems, so Lance is looking to Houghton Ford in Cannington for a trade-in replacement. After discussions with the dealership he decided to but the new Ford 4000, as it fits our work the best. It's a bit more powerful than the old Fordson, and Lance believes that it will do.

Lorna is in hospital in October of 1964 with the birth of their first child. Susan is a lovely little girl who seems to be very relaxed and doesn't seem to make much fuss. With Lorna's training as a mothercraft nurse at N'Gala helps her a lot with her newborn.

The summer is always very busy for us. On Saturdays after the morning milking when the weather suits, Lance takes us down to Rockingham with the boat where the boys have learned to ski. Bill and Janet Robinson have their big boat there too. Keith and Kitt Nicholls and their two boys, Don and Ian are frequently with us too and we do so enjoy that time with everyone. It comes a time when our small boat just isn't big enough anymore so we bought ourselves a new Glasscraft boat with a 40 horsepower outboard motor. Now the boys can learn to ski on just one ski and upgrade their skills.

Our CWA rooms have served us very well as our rest room and meeting room for many years. The curtains which are hanging at the windows are looking a little drab. I purchase some new material and after some careful measuring, make a set of new curtains with some suitably bright coloured material. They do look such a treat as they hang up for the first time.

Keith Marsh and Lance have been working closely together in the Farmers Union for some time. They take some time off from the farm and fly off to Sydney where they have further discussion about the bulk handling of milk in Western Australia. They visit several dairies to form a plan for the introduction of bulk milk handling here in the west.

It must be the year for travel as Marjory and Greg decide to have a holiday before they begin their new business in Newdegate. They board the ship Acadia in Fremantle in May and travel to Melbourne where they spend some time looking around.

Our fawn Falcon sedan has travelled just over its thirty thousand miles in the last two years so Lance is off to buy a replacement. He carefully looks around several of the dealers and decides that we should have something just a bit better than the Ford Falcon, so he buys a Chevrolet Bel-Air. It is such a lovely car to ride in, it seems to just glide over the rougher roads. It is a bit more powerful too with its V8 engine. But after a few months the shine comes off the new car as it starts to rattle. The dealer is unable to find the cause of the rattles after many visits to them in the city. Such a disappointment as we thought we were getting something better than the Falcon.

A few weeks after we bought the Chev, our telephone system is upgraded to an automatic service through the Serpentine exchange. Prior to this we had to contend with the manual service at the Keysbrook exchange which only operated for 12 hours a day. This new service is 24 hours a day and so much easier to use. Rather than the old handle that we used to have to wind up to get connected to the exchange, then ask for the number that we want, we can now just dial our numbers direct. It is so much better than having someone else listening in on our conversations.

Marjory and Greg have begun their business in Newdegate. We have stood as guarantors for them so that they could raise all of the capital from the bank that it would take to set up the business. They have a fuel delivery outlet and a machinery dealership. They have a Bedford truck with fuel tanks on the back and Greg has the job of carting fuel from Lake Grace to the farms that are in the district. They also supply several of the roadhouses with their fuel too. Marjory is mostly busy in the shop and office selling bits and pieces to the farmers and townspeople. They sell firearms too.

The old Horwood-Bagshaw super spreader that we have been using for years is like the rest of us, getting old. Lance has modified it so that it will hold more super but it is so slow at the job. A manufacturer near Redcliff in the city has advertised that he has the best spreader on the market so Lance decides to buy one. Once we get it on the farm he and David set about checking just how good this machine is. They spread out small containers across the path of the spreader and make several passes in the same direction. Most of the super is being spread on one side and they decide that that is not good enough, so we send it back and get our money refunded. They need to do more work on it if they want their machine to be sold to other farmers.

Marjory stops work for a while as she goes into hospital to have her second child. Rodney is born later on in September of 1965. Such a lovely little chap as he lays there in his crib as we watch him through the window of the nursery of the hospital. She is out of hospital soon and after a week or so is at home is back in the shop again with the two little boys to attend to as well.

We all gather at our home for Christmas like we do every year but now our family had grown some. With Gwen's three children, Marjory's two and Lorna's Susan, the family is growing and our Christmas celebrations are taking on a new meaning with these changes. We have room for everyone at the moment and everyone gets along just fine. Lance has made a table tennis table that fits into the car garage and there is always a competition on to see who will beat the others. Sometimes that beastly easterly wind causes some difficulty with the light ball so the doors are lowered to keep the wind out.

Now that David has completed his education he is working with us on the farm. Several of our staff have changed but we still need at least two men to work in the dairy and attend to the other farm duties between milkings.

The horses that we used to use for stock work are reduced to just one horse and old Sandy and David don't seem to get along together too well. We think that we must become modern and move with the times so we purchased a little motor bike for David to use on the farm. The Suzuki comes from Mortlock's in hay Street and seems to do the job well. David says that at least it doesn't need feeding while you are not using it and you don't have to run around for half an hour try to catch the stupid thing when there's stock work to do.

I don't like driving such a large car as the Chev, so we have bought a Ford Cortina for me to drive around in. It will also be available for David when he needs a vehicle to get around in. At present he uses the bike but I don't like it too much as he goes so fast.

A property just a few mile south of the main farm has come on the market. It is just down Utley road and consists of 100 acres to the south of the road with a house and old dairy on it and 200 acres to the north of the road and is pastured but has no improvements on it. It is owned by the Arndt family and Frank wishes to move on and retire. We have a discussion about the farm after looking over it and decide to buy the farm in David's name. It would be good for him to have a good start in life with a solid background of some property. Over the next few years, we replace the boundary fences and remove many of the broken down internal fences and make it a good little block.

Our machinery shed which Lance build near our new home is now just not large enough and we need some more roof area to cover our equipment. Lance and David collect some materials from P&F Supplies in Cannington and get to work building a new Cyclone shed. This is now large enough to take the truck, tractor and my car with some spare room.

As happened with radio in the 1930's, television is now available and after visiting Baird's in the city we bought a new television. The men came out from Baird's and install it for us. The rooftop antenna is attached to the chimney to get the best reception but on some days it can be very "snowy". There are about 4 black and white channels to choose from but Lance likes the news on the ABC and several of their programs.

Our local little CWA group has the opportunity to visit the Mills and Wares biscuit factory in South Terrace, South Fremantle. Here 90% of the workforce are women with many of them having been born overseas. It is such a large setup and it is great to see how our biscuits and cakes are made. I bought home a 10 pound tin of the gingernuts that everyone likes so much.

The little motor bike that we bought for the farm has worn out so it's back to Mortlock's to get a bigger and better one. This is more suited to farm work because it has a slow gear for following cattle.

Lance and the Farmers Union have been pushing for the introduction of bulk milk collection from the farm gate. We had the opportunity to have a look at one of the tankers that Masters would be using for that collection. A semi-trailer with a stainless steel tank with a pump mounted at the back with hoses to make the connection from the truck to the farmer's bulk tank. We visit this at Masters Milk factory just off Stirling Highway.

Our 500 gallon bulk tank arrives and we have trouble getting it into the milk room. The door is too narrow. David removed the roller door and the tracks and a few bricks and with a bit of jostling it slid through. Then it needed to be stood upright and it took the four men to do that. The installers soon had the pipework attached to the freezer unit which they had put in the day before. They had it running just before milking was to begin, so on 28th June 1967 our first pick up of bulk milk occurred. Lance seems so proud as it had taken his efforts and the efforts of the Farmers Union for so many years to convince the milk factories that this is the best method of handling milk at the farm gate.

A few months later Marjory has another mouth to feed. Their son Craig was born to them in September 1967. He had light coloured curly hair and it is such a joy to see Marjory so happy with her boys.

Lance and I had taken the caravan for a short trip to visit Marjory and Greg and were away from the farm for a few days in early December. Neil, David and his fiancé Barbara, had taken the boat down to Rockingham for a skiing session. They were on their way home and noticed a large plume of smoke to the east of the road they were on. They reckoned that the smoke must be coming from somewhere near the farm. They hurried home and found that the back paddock of Hectors block was on fire. The men had taken a tractor and plough and made some firebreaks and some locals were there with their fire units too. David and Neil headed to the fire with our fire unit and with everyone's help was able to stop the fire just after it had entered Fletchers place and burnt down his 4000 bale haystack. The men took to the milking while David and Barbara waited by our haystack to put out the rolling cowpats that were spreading sparks across the ground towards our haystack, which was in the middle of the burnt paddock. During the evening it rained. Neil called us as soon as knew what was happening and we hurried home and got there just after dark.

Towards the end of 1966, Neil completed his education and he also came to work on the farm with his Father and brother. The boys and their father worked together with Neil being able to fit into the jobs that David wasn't able to do.

At our CWA annual elections, I was returned as president once again and this time Faye Kite is the treasurer. The next month I had arranged through Lorna to visit her as she worked at N'Gala. It was eye opening for so many of our ladies to see so many babies and little children in the one place being cared for by such a lovely group of young ladies.

David has been attending youth club in Serpentine, where he made some friends and meets with some of his old school mates. There are several girls there too and he takes a shine to one of them. Barbara McKay's father is a prison officer and they live at Karnet, not far from our home, just up the hill. She is the manageress at "Tom the Cheep" Grocer at his Pinjarra shop and travels right past our front gate twice a day. They have been going together for several months and on 11th of April they announced their engagement.

The old house by the railway line that we use as a staff house has reached the end of its life. With the cost of building a new house so expensive we looked at Alco who build houses in their factory and deliver them on trucks to the site. They built for us a two bedroom house with dining area, kitchen, bathroom and laundry. Lance extended the power line down to the cottage so it would be a bit more comfortable for the staff family.

The 19th October 1968 was a special day as that is when our eldest son, David become married to his fiancé Barbara. The wedding is in the Byford Presbyterian Church with the reception held in the Armadale Lesser Hall. There was such a large gathering of friends and family. Young Stephen was their page boy with little Susan being the flower girl. It was a lovely day and everything went off as planned. We didn't have a house for them to live in, so arranged for them to live in Bill and Janet Robinson's farm house. Several months after they moved into the house on the block we bought from Hectors. It is complete with 32 volt system and a couple of kerosene fridges.

Lorna has given birth for her second time. Another lovely daughter. Diane is an energetic little one with her mother's darker hair.

David and Barbara have their first child. A boy. Kevin will be able to carry on the Kentish name and this makes us so proud

Within a few weeks of each other, little Wayne is born to Marjory and Greg, who are still at Newdegate. He seems to have some issue with his legs but this does not cause him any permanent difficulty.

Greg and Marjory's business is not as profitable as they made us believe in spite of Lance asking at every opportunity. Greg seemed to always be a bit evasive when we ask how it's all going. He leads us to believe that they are doing well and have more money coming in than going out. It was only a few weeks later that we get notified by the bank that they were not making their payments on the loans for which we had stood as guarantors. A short time later Greg flies out to East Africa and leaves Marjory to take care of the boys.

Lance has had enough of the rattles of the Chev so he buys a new Ford Fairlane 500. He is so glad to be back at home with a Ford in the shed.

David and Barbara work together on the farm particularly when there is stock work to do. They were down at Arndt's moving some young stock to the other side when David had an accident on the motorbike. The front wheel went down a hollow and collided with a stump on the other side which could not be seen in the long grass. Neither he nor the bike suffered any long term damage or injury but it did scare us all.

We are finding that the storage tanks that we have for our household, stock and dairy water are not large enough. We used to pump water from the creek up until Christmas but this now dries up much earlier. The new shed that houses my little Cortina and the new truck catches a lot of rain water and we have a new concrete tank built to hold that water. Lance soon has the pipework connected up so it all works well.

Before the hay season in 1969 we moved away from the old conventional mowers and purchased a new rotary slasher mower. This will allow David to cut the hay a lot faster.

With the new three and a half ton Marshal super spreader the old Bedford was not large enough to do the job. The bulk bin that we bought some months ago and fitted on the back of the Bedford could not be filled to make the best use of Lance's time in carting super. A Dodge 690 was bought and this allowed Lance to cart 7 tons of super at a time. So two fills of the super spreader and he needs to collect another load.

The old stock crate that fitted the Bedford was modified to fit the Dodge so it can carry twice as many cows as before.

Before Christmas our CWA held its meeting in our home again as the ladies had prepared our Christmas events. The decoration that we used were left in place so we could enjoy them for our family Christmas too. Our Christmas together as a family is growing even larger. Marjory is here with her four boys, and Lorna is here with her two girls and David's Barbara is here with their little one. We have a grand time with all of the little ones whose ages are similar, all running around the back yard and playing together.

A week or so later Marjory puts her four boys onto a plane and head off to Kenya to meet up with Greg who has a house ready for them. He has been employed by a machinery dealership and is liking the climate.

Barbara is elected to the position of treasurer of the CWA as she has been a member for six months or more. With her bookkeeping skills, she soon has the books in order.

We have had Fordson and Ford Dexta tractors here on our farm for many years and this year we need to replace the larger one. Lance and David decide that we need to improve and select a four wheel drive Zetor tractor for the super spreading and forage harvesting.

Chapter 19

I have been busy again with my craft work that keeps my mind and fingers active. I have some coloured beads that I make into little brooches with a short piece of fine wire to keep them all together. I have been busy with my crocheting in the evenings too as we watch television together. Now that the girls and David have left the family home it is Just Lance, Neil and myself here, so I like to keep myself busy. It seems that I have been like this all my life and I just am not able to be sitting around. Crocheting, craft and knitting keeps my hands and mind busy. I also have been making some carry bags for shopping and storing my knitting projects in. Mummy Gomm taught me how to do so much when I was looking after her and Pop and I have been busy at those things ever since.

I usually have a little mystery prize at the CWA meetings where I can have someone else enjoy the fruits of my work. Barbara won one of the brooches early in March 1970. She has kept that little memento for many years.

June 1970 sees our little Keysbrook CWA group of ladies together for 21 years. We consider this to be a new milestone for us. We have had so many laughs, learnt so many things and developed so many skills over the years that I can't remember them all. We hold our 21st birthday party in our restrooms, which used to be the old Keysbrook state school so many years ago. We have made it so much more comfortable over the years and now it seems like it's part of us.

Clem's dairy is on the home block and his dairy cows like to graze on the paddocks just over the railway line. They have been working with the railway people all this time with no incidents but this one day it all went wrong. There was an unscheduled freight train service that happened to coincide with him taking his dairy herd across the Bunbury Highway and then across the railway line. Half of the herd was across when the train hit them. He tried to separate the herd but they were in a hurry to get to the pasture and didn't like being stopped. He lost 11 of his best cows that day. He was so angry. He protested with the railways but they would not listen, that is their right of way and he'd just have to live with it.

David's asthma was affected by the wet winters and also during the spring. Some days he was too ill to work and some days he wished he didn't but he survived. Mowing for meadow hay was particularly difficult as he got to the stage where his eyes would close up and he could barely see. The doctor prescribed drugs to offset the effects but although these made him sleepy he needed to take them. The oats dust in the dairy was very bad and on some days he wore a breathing apparatus. He had many discussions with Lance about the methods he was using as David had been shown more up to date methods at Narrogin. This caused some conflicts as Lance was fairly set in his ways and was difficult to convince of change.

David and Lance have not been entirely happy working together for some time. One day when Lance was at their home an argument erupted and David would not take any more from Lance so he, his wife Barbara and son Kevin, decided to leave the farm. They have moved to Mandurah in their caravan and found work with a builder. Lance tries to encourage them back but they are adamant that they will stand by their decision. A month or so later they do call in on their way north to find a place to settle in.

At our September CWA meeting I was able to play a tape recording which I had received from Marjory who is in Kenya. She described their life there and how the boys loved to see the animals that are so much different from those back home. It was lovely to hear her voice. But she was soon to return home again with her four boys and with no money. Our old "Wee Hoos" on Bolinda Vale, the original Kentish farm, by the creek was empty so Clem allowed them to stay there until they could get on their feet. It was great for the boys as they could take part in some farm activities. Marjory would help out on Clem's farm and also our farm when we had special stock or farm work to be done.

Neil usually meets up with Colin on the weekends. Neil had not heard from him at the time when Colin was supposed to visit. He phoned Ira who said that he was in the shed out the back and perhaps Neil should come over there to see him. Neil drove over and on entering the shed could hear the grinder going but found Colin lying on the floor with an obvious head injury. They called for the ambulance which rushed him to hospital. They were able to save his life but the head injury was disastrous. Clem and Ira have tried every avenue of surgery and care for Colin since but he was never able to be the same bright young lad that he was.

David, Barbara and young Kevin lived in Carnarvon for about a year and while working for a water boring contractor, move to his base in Geraldton and soon after bought a house. They had been in the house for about five months when their second child, Bruce was born. David had to leave to return to Carnarvon with his work soon after Barbara returned home from hospital.

Ira is in a tizz. Coralie is about to be married to Graham in July 1970 and they are in the last stages of planning the wedding. I remember Clem walking Coralie down the aisle with a very proud look on his face. But it all goes off without a hitch and after a short honeymoon they return to work on their farm.

My brother Don and his family have been living in Geraldton for some time and have a nice home there. Don died of a stroke in March 1974 and we drove up to attend his funeral. We visited their home afterwards with David & Barbara but they didn't know each other in spite of living in the same town. Don and Vesper were of the Jehovah's Witness religious sect and Lance did not seem to be able to accept the fact, so it made visiting my brother difficult in years past.

Just some three months later, Gwen is in hospital again, this time giving birth to her baby, Jim. She was 36 at the time. That gives them two boys and two girls to make a great family. They have been living at their farming property at Coogely Hills just north of Mardella for several years.

In 1976 the Kentish family have been on the Bolinda Vale farm for 50 years. They had travelled overland from Boolaroo in South Australia in 1926, searching for greener pastures. To celebrate the event we, Ira, Clem, Lance, Enid, Esther and I organise a "Back to Keysbrook" event. It was a lovely day and it was great to see so many people attending and remembering some of the old times that we all used to share.

There have been difficulties in the dairy industry and with the problem with staff and Lance getting on in years, we made the decision to quit the dairy. After the mornings milking in June 1976 with the help of a few stock trucks we take the dairy herd to the Mundijong saleyards where the agents have organised a sale for us. It was successful with all of the stock, mostly Australian Illawarra Shorthorns being sold. The dairy was cleaned out and the milking equipment sold off too. The shed was to sit idle for a time before any decision was made of what to do with it.

Marjory had been divorced from Greg for several years and she began working for a fuel merchant in Forrestfield. Ken had several daughters and Marjory took a liking to them and him. Soon they are to be married and this was a quiet affair in February 1977. She moved in with them with her four boys to make a big family.

David and Barbara have begun their own business in Geraldton and have sold their home in the Geraldton suburb of Tarcoola and bought a few acres along the Mullewa road just a few kilometres from town. They operate their crane, windmill and bore business from there and have plenty of room for the boys to run around or ride their bikes. Vicki was born in February 1977, four months after they had shifted in.

Gwen's second daughter, Doreen and Garry married in January 1980 while they had the Perth Tourist Caravan Park. Gwen and Fred moved to a new house down the side street while Doreen and Garry took the main house as part of the caravan park.

Neil has become engaged to Jacky whose parents moved from England several years before. They have set a wedding day and we have decided that they will be able to live in the family home and we would build ourselves a new home in Armadale. With the help of Lorna and Barry who have redeveloped their orchard property into housing, we were able to have our house built not far from them. We took some time to consider what we wanted and no steps was the main requirement as both of us are getting on and we should be making things easier not more difficult. The brick and tile house was finished several weeks before the wedding and after we moved in Neil needed to batch for the remaining time.

Neil and Jacky's wedding ceremony was held in Jacky's family back yard and the reception in the Gypsy Baron Restaurant in Armadale. It was a lovely affair with so many new faces and friends to meet. We would have preferred that they had their wedding in a church but neither of Jackie's parents were very religious so they settled for a garden wedding in the home in Forrestfield. The reception saw so many more of our local people and more new friends that we had not met before being present to wish them well for their future together. David, Barbara and family came down from Geraldton for the event and it was a good opportunity to talk with them for a while too.

Although we are living in Armadale, Lance still went to the farm most days to help Neil with what jobs were necessary. As the years progressed his ability to work reduced and Neil was able to do more of the work by himself and with employees from time to time. One of Lance's favourite jobs was to use his ride-on mower to clear the grass away from fences and buildings. He had an accident and cut his fingers when he tried to remove some sticks from under the mower. The fingers never mended properly and were a problem for the rest of his life. He also like to use the rode-on mower to mow the grass on the council park which is alongside our home. We even had a bore put down and some underground sprinklers fitted in so Lance needed to spend less time with the garden and lawn.

Gwen's eldest son Eric marries his sweetheart, Susan in a delightful ceremony in the middle of November of 1981.

Neil is working with his beef cattle but has some sheep as well and needed a shearing shed, so he converted the dairy for this purpose. The raised concrete floor was covered and pens built. A grated floor, was fitted over a section for the sheep pens. The rest was covered in plywood flooring to form the area where the shearers would work and for the wool handling area.

During the time we lived at Mount View I had developed a grand garden with hydrangeas along the edge of the verandah on the south side. Just out from the dining room window was a bed of roses. Beside them was my kitchen garden. I use to grow all manner of vegetable here. Peas, strawberries, cucumbers and so on and an apricot tree. They used to grow very well with some cow manure from the dairy. I was just so disappointed that when Neil and Jacky moved in, the garden was destroyed as this didn't fit in with Jacky's plans.

October 1981 saw us once again attend the garden party at Government House to visit with the Queen and Prince Philip. It was a grand affair with everyone dressed in their finest attire. Prince Philip made a few jokes which made everyone laugh. We met with the Governor General and so many other dignitaries that I just don't remember their names. But we did enjoy our time there.

Lance is complaining about his eyesight. He used to be able to see very well but lately it seem his vision has blurred and he is having some level of difficulty with his reading. We visit the optician and he carries out his tests after we discuss the situation with Doctor Plozza. He'll need new glasses and we have some drops to put in his eyes several times a day. Soon he can see betted but not as well as before.

The government keeps changing the rules regarding our pension and it is becoming so difficult to keep it sorted out so that we can get from them what they offer and say that we should be getting. We have to visit their office once again and wait in line until our number is called out. We sit with their lady for a while and she assures us that the problems have been fixed and that we will not have any more problems with our pension. During 1983, in recognition of his service to the community, Clem was honoured by being recognised as the first Honorary Freeman of the Shire of Serpentine-Jarrahdale. He has spent so much time and effort with the Serpentine Jarrahdale Roads Board and following the change to shire councils, he continued with the Shire Council of Serpentine-Jarrahdale. While he and Ira were holidaying in Africa the new hall was named in Serpentine. Eric Senior, the vice president made sure that the new hall would bear his name. So it is now known as the Clem Kentish Hall.

Chapter 20

While sitting at the breakfast table one morning I noticed that Lance was having some problems. His speech was slurred and he seemed confused. He tried to stand but lost his balance and sat back onto the chair. I was frightened for him as I didn't know what to make of it so I phoned the doctor and booked him in for a visit for just after lunch time. After asking him some questions and doing a few tests, he came back to us and told us that Lance had had a small stroke. This condition may also affect his eyesight so we booked in to see the optician for the next week. Further tests have shown that he may have had several of these strokes previously and not recognised the symptoms.

Neil and Jacky's first born arrived in March of 1983. Josephine is a bonny little baby who always seems to be happy and contented.

Jacky's father and mother have moved from their home in Forrestfield to live in the house on Hectors block, where David and Barbara had lived for a while. After some careful renovations, Jack has made it a much more comfortable home for them. He also is a big help around the farm for Neil as he gets involved in planting trees or as he calls it Agroforestry. Jack also helped Neil to develop some machinery for handling rolls of hay and a gauge for indicating the water level in tanks.

Lance has put up with the pains in his forehead for many years and recently has had the problem diagnosed as sinusitis. The doctors have had him on antibiotics and other medication for some time but the problem still persists. When we were younger and busy all the time, we put up with these problems but now that we aren't so busy with business and farm activity the problems seem so much more persistent. The doctor has him admitted to Rockingham hospital where they carry out an operation to remove some bone from his forehead to allow the sinus fluid to flow more freely. He was out of hospital after several days and once the swelling had gone down, the problem has almost cleared up.

Florrie and Harrold had been living in Chidlow for many years but in more recent times they had moved to live in Middle Swan, not far from Midland. Harold passed away in August of 1983.

Lance is still busy with the Mofflyn Children's Home. He has been on the board for that Christian organisation for so many years that I can't count them. He attends their meetings in Victoria Park near the city several times each year to help keep things running as smoothly as possible. Mofflyn does so much good work with the homeless and "at danger" children. There are the several homes to take care of some children and there are other cottages to provide care for several others as well.

I have been having a lot of discomfort in my legs lately and they feel heavy. Sometimes it feels like a burning sensation and sometimes itchy. The doctor examined my legs and determined that even though they can't be easily seen, I have varicose veins. The doctors suggested that I could lose some weight, which might help. I could wear some compression stockings that might help too. I am trying both so we'll see just how well that works.

Lance spends some days on the farm with Neil. One day he is checking some stock on the North Dandalup property. The turn off to the gateway is partway down a hill on a two lane road. He had slowed down before he got to the gate as he was looking at the cattle in the paddock and a few cars lined up behind him. The road markings showed that they could not overtake him at this point. Just before the gateway he turned on his indicators and moved to the right side of the road. Unbeknown to him there was another car travelling at speed overtaking the line of cars which had accumulated behind him in his Landcruiser. He was almost across the other side of the road with the front wheels on the gravel when the other car hit. The crash caused the Landcruiser to spin around forcing Lance hard into his seatbelt. His car ended up in the gateway and the other vehicle in the ditch. Both cars were written off by their insurance companies and the driver faced time in court because he was inattentive while driving or some such error. Lance was bruised and was quite sore for several days. He was shaken up but this did not stop his love for driving. After the insurance payout he was able to buy a new Toyota Silver Series four wheel drive wagon.

Several months after this I was suffering from a fever and a swollen face that would not seem to go away. The doctor admitted me to hospital where they did some tests to find the cause. He gave me some medication and the fever went away after a few days and the swelling slowly subsided.

Before I went into hospital we had ordered a new caravan from the dealer on the highway in Maddington. It was ready for us to pick up near the end of March 1984. It was lovely and had all the modern things in it like a toilet and shower. The bed was very comfortable and Lance told me that it towed very well. We did many trips with that van and we so enjoyed our time with friends and travelling around seeing all of the sights to see that are around us.

A month after we picked up our new caravan the trip that we had booked on last year, was ready for us. Lorna took us to the airport where we boarded a plane for Sydney. We were picked up by a coach from the airport and delivered to the harbour where we boarded our cruise ship that would take us on a cruise around the Pacific and the many islands which are there. It was very busy on the wharf with so many people wanting to get on board. We waited patiently and soon we were moving up the gangway. One of the staff showed us to our cabin that we were to stay in for the trip. We departed the harbour during the evening and the ship was steady until we got out to sea and then it began a gentle roll. After dinner in the restaurant we talked with some other folk for a while before heading off to bed. It had been a very long day and in spite of the ship's movement we slept very soundly. Our first port of call on the second day was Suva, Fiji. Near midday we had an onshore excursion and visited so many of the tourist areas of the town and surrounds. They have such lovely gardens here with such a range of colourful flowers and plants. We couldn't stay too long as the ship had to leave before dark to get on its way to the next destination. Such a pretty little place to visit. Our next stop is the Port of Lautoka which is on the other side of the island of Fiji. This place was similar in many ways as Suva but a little more relaxed. Just as hilly when away from the coastal areas.

Back on board again and we head west and visit Noumea which is in New Caledonia. Such pretty country out here, almost unbelievable with the mountains, the colourful water and gardens and clean beaches. We are surprised by a dance from one of the local groups of ladies in their grass skirts with the men beating on the drums. We had such a lovely day, it was a pity for it to end. Our next port that we enter is Honiara on the big island of Guadalcanal in the

Solomon Islands. Then it's on to Vila in Vanuatu. This is such a lovely small island where they have around two thousand earth tremors here each year. We felt a small one while we were on land and that was quite unnerving. Not as bad as the Meckering earth quake back in 1968 but still enough to shake things up a bit. From here we travel back to Noumea before returning to Sydney.

It was such an enjoyable two weeks on the cruise but we were ready to step onto firm ground again. After spending a night in a hotel we are back on a flight that would take us home again. The memories of that trip will stay with me for ever.

We support Marjory as much as we can and in the middle of 1984, we took a trip to Exmouth. Marjory had travelled by bus and we picked her up from Carnarvon. This is during the "dry" season but the weather must have become confused because it rained. It rained so heavy that we got washed out of the caravan park in Exmouth. She stayed with us for a few days and on the way back to the highway to take her to the bus stop, we had to pull a car out of the mud as they had driven off the road. It was a lovely few days together in spite of the rainy weather. I did have an issue one night with chest pains. I didn't want to wake Marjory and slowly the pains subsided and that allowed me to become more comfortable again.

In the middle of November in 1984, Neil is preparing to take on more responsibility at the farm. We sign a contract with him that allows him to have more control over several of the blocks. He has bought a couple of new John Deere tractors after he sold one of the blocks he had bought from us with his mortgage.

Audrey, Gwen's eldest daughter and Linton have their wedding day just a month before Christmas in 1984.

In the middle of December 1984 Neil and Jacky are blessed with the arrival of their son Stuart into this world. Such a bonny little chap and a little brother for Josephine.

Dorothy and Abel have retired from their farm and have been living near Denmark, lower in the southwest for several years. Abel has not been well for a time and he passed away in the middle of May 1985.

Neil wants to use the old dairy for the purpose of shearing. He has used it before but it is not really suited for that purpose. After some discussion we work out a plan and gift him about $8000 so he can improve the grating and the plywood floor to make it more suitable.

Lorna and Barry's eldest daughter, Susan was married today to Peter at a lovely ceremony in Kelmscott. 12th October 1985 was such a memorable day.

Lance is having more difficulty at times with his balance so to help with this problem we have bought a "Wheelie Walker", which his sister Esther has been selling. It allows him to move around more easily and gives him some support when he gets tired. But I wish he wouldn't leave it in my way so often.

Just before Christmas in 1985 young Kevin arrives down from Geraldton and Lance and I drive to the bus depot to pick him up as he is staying with us for a week or so. During the next week or so Lance and Kevin help Neil in his newly modified shearing shed. Lance says that it works well enough but could be better.

Harold Boas Park is near the city behind the Parliament House on Havelock Street. This was the site of Marjory's eldest son, Stephen and his lady Cheryl's wedding in November 1986. It was a lovely setting, out amongst the gardens and flowers

In March of 1987 we celebrate our Golden Wedding Anniversary in the CWA rooms in Armadale. Gwen and Fred were there with most of their children, Marjory was there with several of her boys. Lorna and Barry attended too with Susan, Peter and Diane. David and Barbara had travelled down from Geraldton with their two boys and Vicki. Neil and Jacky were there as well with their two little ones. We were able to assemble the original wedding group with Clem and Keith, Connie and Esther. And so many others that I may have forgotten to mention. It was such a lovely day. Clem is still up to his old pranks. He gives us a tin of Golden Syrup as a celebratory gift. It seems he thought it must have been fitting. Lance was just a bit taken aback by this gesture but we accepted it in good faith.

In June 1987 we take another caravan trip. We find a few nice places to stop in for the night as we head up north. We spend a few days with David, Barbara and their family in Geraldton. They had just returned home from a short trip to Singapore and they showed us some photos and David's new camera. Then we travel on to Carnarvon. After spending a few days here we visit Bush Bay for a few days on the way home again. When we return to Janalli Way we find that while we were away we have been broken into again. One of the back windows has been forced open and they came in through that. We call the police but they either can't do anything or find it all a bit too hard. It is so depressing to have our lovely home broken into again and this upsets both of us quite a bit. We find that as well as some money was taken, they also scattered our paperwork all around the room. They were obviously looking for more.

After some discussion we ask Barry and Brian to organise the fitting of window locks to help make the place more secure.

Lance seems to be deteriorating in his ability to some of the more difficult tasks. He needs my help now to connect the van onto the car. He had always done it by himself but now relies more on my help to get the jolly things together.

My shoulders are giving me some trouble and it seems that I need some help too. The vacuuming is difficult but I am determined not to allow the discomfort to stop me from doing the simple things that I have been doing all of my life.

It has come time for me to be tested for my driver's licence again. I passed with flying colours, so that is another little problem that I don't have to face for some time. Everyone on the road can be satisfied that they will be safe from me for the time being.

Chapter 21

Several of the younger ones in the Lavis family have organised a family reunion to be held in King's Park early in December 1987. I wasn't too sure just how it would all turn out so I invited all of our family to attend. David, Barbara and their family were able to attend all the way from Geraldton. Gwen and Fred, Marjory, Lorna and Barry were there. It was such an excellent day and the weather was kind to us as well. We make up such a large group and it was so exciting to catch up with so many of my sisters and brother all at the same time again.

On New Year's Eve the cover that I put over my lovely new Cressida is stolen during the night. It is just so disappointing that someone should do such a thing. If someone was in trouble they could just ask for help. It is just beyond my thinking that they should just take something which is not theirs.

A relative of Lances has been spending a lot of time researching and assembling a lot of detail of the Kentish family. Peter Kentish and several helpers invited all of the Kentish's in Australia to attend a family reunion in Adelaide in April 1988. We travelled over on the train and had such a lovely trip with the staff being very helpful. We stayed with a pair of Lance's cousins Win and Hazel, who lived in Adelaide. Gwen and Fred drove over with their caravan in tow. David, Barbara

and little Vicki drove over with their caravan from
Geraldton. Clem and Ira were travelling around the
eastern states in their caravan so they were able to be
there too. It was such a grand event meeting up with so
many of the family members who Lance had been
talking about all of these years. It was so nice to be able
to put a face to the names. Also we were able to talk
with so many of the family from the east who had been
able to visit us in the west.

The meetings took place over several days of the Easter
period. We went to church on the Sunday as so many of
the family were there too. So much information was
provided for us along with some paperwork showing
how all of the family members are joined up to those
who arrived in South Australia during 1838. It was very
informative and thoroughly enjoyable to meet up with
so many. But like all good things, the weekend must
come to an end. After a picnic in the park we all go our
separate ways and next day we are back on the train
again heading home. Lance does enjoy the train ride as
he can just sit back and let someone else do the work for
a change.

A few weeks later have a visit from Neil. He wants to
buy the home farm so that he can do more with it than
he is able to as a lessee. Over the next weeks we work
out a suitable deal and after he approaches his bank we
settle. He and Jacky are now the owners of Mount View.
He has plans to extend his agroforestry and carry out

more of the grading that has proved successful over the last few years. We see this as a positive step forward for the farm.

We watch the Commonwealth Games that are held in Canada on the television. Audrey, Gwen's eldest daughter has been playing badminton ever since she could hold a racquet. She has competed in several other Commonwealth games events with some very good results in the past and now she is playing in the Olympics and is doing so very well.

We do our weekly shopping in the new shopping centre in Armadale. We don't take very long these days as there is just the two of us in the house and we don't have big appetites any more. We had been away from our home for just forty five minutes and on our return, we find that one of our windows was smashed and someone had broken in again. They have stolen our tape recorder and many of our papers have gone too. Just as well that we keep our important papers with the bank for safe keeping. Barry and Brian once again are asked to help and this time we have all of our windows fitted with strong security mesh. It seems that this lovely location is not as secure as it should be for older folks like us. Our lovely home now feels and looks like a prison. We are so disappointed about that and the fact that the police have not caught anyone yet.

Lance has had a few close calls with his driving lately and after talking with his doctor it was decided that his driver's licence should not be renewed. He has had a good driving records since he was old enough to drive on the farm at the age of ten, so this came as a big blow to him. He feels that his independence has been eroded away.

Now that our house is fortified like a prison the next damage is to our shed. The large door had been smashed and some tools and gear has been stolen from the storage area and cupboard.

In December 1988, the optician has me booked in to the hospital to have cataracts removed from my eyes. They'll do one for now and in a few weeks' time they will do the same op to the other. St John of God hospital in Subiaco is such a big place now but the nurses were very helpful. I was out of there about lunch time.

Lance is having trouble with his waterworks and after some tests done by the doctor it is decided that he would need an operation. Towards the end of June 1989 he is admitted to the hospital in Armadale. Apparently his prostate gland has some problems so they will need to do surgery to determine what needs to be done. They remove a part of the gland which had become cancerous. He had a lot of bruising on his lower body and he took a few days to recover before being allowed to return home again.

My lovely little sister Margaret who married John Lambie and later Tom Daw many years after John had died, has been ill and in hospital for several sessions with an ongoing illness. After a fight to stay in this world she passed away in August 1989. It was so difficult for so many of us at the funeral service where we went to respect her life and say our final farewells. She is with God now and at peace at last.

It is such a lovely few months when we have so many weddings. All of our grand-children are moving forwards with their lives.

Diane, Lorna's daughter, marries Glen in a lovely ceremony with the reception being held in the dining room at Araluen where we have spent so many lovely visits when the flowers and tulips are blooming. Lance said the grace before the meal and had a little emotional session. That was in October 1989.

Just a few weeks later her cousin Rodney, married his Jacky in another lovely ceremony.

Lance had been trying to get me to ride a bicycle for many years and we went to the local bike shop to talk about a new push-bike each. Lance bought a comfortable two wheeler with gears and I chose to buy a bike with one wheel at the front and two wheels at the back with a little basket on the frame between the wheels.

NOW I CAN RIDE!

Every day we take some time to ride around the streets and paths close to home and thoroughly enjoy ourselves. I don't know why we didn't do this years ago. Lance falls from his bike several times but as he had been riding since he could walk he didn't seem to hurt himself very much.

Before the end of November 1989 we pay for our burial plots in the Serpentine cemetery. The plot that we have chosen is right beside Lance's parents grave. We know our time is not in the distant future so we plan ahead for the final event.

In 1989 Clem resigned his position on the Council of the Serpentine Jarrahdale Shire. A record of forty seven years as both Roads Board Member and Shire Councillor, one year as Chairman of the local Roads Board and twenty six years as the Shire President of the Serpentine Jarrahdale Shire. At the age of seventy five, Clem needed to slow down a bit and allow some other members of the community to carry on with that work which he had been doing within the district.

Our friend George Marriot who had visited the farm during the war years when his army unit was based near Mundijong, had not been very well for a few months. He and Enid have had many years together and had visited us on many occasions. We would visit them on their vegetable farm in the hills near Melbourne whenever we had the chance to travel over that way. George passed away the day after Christmas Day in 1989.

New Year's Day has been celebrated at Clem and Ira's beach shack on the beach at Mandurah for many years. Each of the family members tries very hard to attend on the day, as do the many friends and neighbours. It's one of the few times each year that many of us are able to meet and this gives everyone a lot of enjoyment.

Neil and Jacky have been playing tennis at the Serpentine club courts for several years and took the opportunity to build their own tennis court just out from the house. They spend many happy hours with friends playing tennis at home.

David and Barbara have sold their business in Geraldton and have moved to Forrestfield where they have a lovely house up on the side of the hills. They can see some of the Perth city from their front area. David has an office job with one of the company's that they worked so well with, in the past.

Lance seems to be have more and more difficulty riding his bike. Some days he would fall off several times seemingly for no reason. He'd lay on the ground for a few minutes then get up again and continue riding. He is very obstinate and refuses to give in. When he falls off I try to do what I can for him but he refuses help.

I talk with Gwen, Marjory, Lorna, David and Neil about what is happening and we decide that perhaps we need to have a family meeting to talk about what is happening and how we can get around the problems. After a lot of discussion at the meeting we decide that the best thing for us to do is to sell our lovely home and move into a retirement home where I can have some help to manage Lance's problems.

Early in February 1990, Lance is having problems again with his water works and after we visit the doctor, an ambulance is ordered to take him into Saint John of God hospital in Riverton so he can have the prostate gland removed altogether. He has the surgery the next day and his recovery takes a week, so it is some time before he is able to return home to me again.

While Lance is in the hospital I look at several option for a retirement home and find a lovely home in the Amaroo village in Kenwick, which is just a few kilometres from our home. I discuss this with Lance while he is in the hospital and he agrees to the idea. Neil is able to spend a little time with me to make an application for us to have a unit at the village.

Lance has been in hospital for sixteen days before he is able to return home. Our plans to go the Amaroo village are progressing but first we have to sell our home.

David and Barbara's son Kevin married Alison in a park in Belmont. Such a nice little area for an outdoor wedding. Their reception was held in a pleasant restaurant in Kenwick called Alfresco Gardens. Well, what a lovely day that turned out to be after a frustrating beginning. I went to the hairdresser and asked Lance to sit on the seat outside while I had my hair done. He seemed a bit off this morning. Nothing particular was wrong but a bit off colour I thought. But when I came out from the hairdresser he was not on the seat. I looked everywhere for him. I called Lorna and she came to help me look too. Apparently he was in a bit of a daze and wandered off. Someone picked him up and asked where he lived and dropped him off at our home address. Lorna and I went home and found him there. He was quite unsure of what had happened. The rest of the day was marvellous.

Near the middle of June after our home had been sold we finalised the deal with the Amaroo Village and we moved in on the 14th. So much furniture that is too big but with a bit of a squeeze we are able to get most of it to fit in. It is such a lovely little place and the ladies on both sides of us are very friendly and helpful. There is a place for me to park my Cressida but the caravan stays at David's new place in Wattle Grove.

Lance is recovering from his operations and now needs vitamin B injections to help him along the way.

Neil is progressing with the farm and wants to do some more development with his agroforestry. He borrows another twenty thousand dollars from us so he is able to finance his project.

My lovely little car had been broken into. The lock on the passenger side was damaged and the sun shade and several small items are missing. Such a shame, as we thought that we had left those problems behind us in Armadale. The police attended and the insurance covered the damage but we still felt so violated with the break-in.

David is now a proud grandfather, as early in August 1990, Kevin's Alison had given him a grandson, Riley Blake. Another one to carry on the family name of Kentish into the future. Riley is one of several who will carry the Kentish name into the future

Lance relinquished his Motor Vehicle Driver's license due to slow reflexes and failing sight several years ago. I would then drive the car with the caravan behind. We did a few trips in this fashion but I was not happy with driving and towing the caravan. Lance was becoming very slow and sometimes needed help to get around and I felt the strain of this extra work.

A month after my car had been burgled the Village management had security cameras fitted around the homes near us so that did make us feel a little more secure.

We take a trip north by bus and meet up with Gwen and Fred in Broome. Fred helped with Lance as he was in a wheelchair for some of the time and the load was proving too much for me. It is such lovely weather in Broome and we find it very relaxing. Lance became very embarrassed when Fred drove us down and along Cable Beach. It seems that some people, mainly women, like to bathe naked in the sun. Fred didn't realise where we were and drove by them with their naked bodies in the sun. Such a sight! Lance was not very impressed and urged Fred to drive on.

Chapter 22

Shortly after our return from the Broome tour, Lance was admitted to the Gosnells Family Hospital. His X-ray results showed that the cancer which was in his prostate had not all been removed and it had flared up again. The doctors did not think that he would recover from this problem.

After a few days he showed no improvement and was allowed to return home for palliative care. By this time he was bed ridden and needed constant attention, so with the help of the Silver Chain Nurses, our children helped to take care of Lance in our home at Amaroo. The cancer that had caused the problem with his prostate had caused him, among other things, to lose the use of his legs. Whilst at home Lance's condition deteriorated quickly and he slipped into a coma. On the 23rd of September 1990, he quietly passed away in our home, with most of our family alongside.

Clem and Ira were touring in their caravan with Hughie and Stella Manning and were able to return home in time to spend a few hours with Lance just prior to his passing. Lorna and Barry were returning from a caravan trip in the eastern states and arrived home a few days just before the funeral.

Lance was buried in the cemetery at Serpentine close to his parents' graves after a very moving Funeral Service at our Congregational Church in Armadale. The

Reverend Terry Tero, who had married David &
Barbara conducted the service. During this service
Marjory and Neil read out the Eulogy which was
prepared by David.

We had been married fifty three and a half years and I
miss him so very much. He was the very strong young
man who was clearing the land with hand tools that I
fell in love with all those years ago. He was my husband
and the father to all of our children and was such a help
in bringing them up. He helped guide me with our
Christian devotions every day. He was the man who sat
beside me at church every Sunday. He was the man
who travelled to so many of the communities around
our home in Keysbrook to take so many Church services
as a Lay preacher. He was the man I loved. He was the
man who helped guide so many young people on the
right path with his work with the Mofflyn Homes. He
was the man who helped the dairy industry in Western
Australia move to bulk milk handling. He was the man
who helped so many people in the Dwellingup bush
fires. He was the man I loved. He was the man who had
the foresight to guide us from near poverty to a level of
affluence. He was the man who gave me what I needed.
He was the man who had very strong ideals. He was the
man I loved.

And I shall miss him so very, very much.

With the help of my children, the Church, God and the
Amaroo community I was able to move on. Very slowly

at first but I gradually began to overcome my grief. It took time but I did feel better after a while. But I was still lonely.

A month after Lance's passing I began to feel unwell with chest pains again and palpitations. I had suffered for years with mild angina and it seems that this has flared up again. The doctor admitted me to hospital and gave me some more medication to help with the problem. This did give me some relief.

I was out again after several days and spent some time with Lorna and Barry. She took care of me very well and it felt good to be pampered a little. I returned home to our little home in Amaroo but it seemed very lonely again.

Near the end of October I was back in hospital again with a severe bout of breathlessness. It seemed like I just could not get enough air into my lungs. The staff at Fremantle Hospital looked after me very well and on my release I spent a few days with Gwen and Fred. I did have a couple of bad nights with no feeling in my left hand. This passed after a time.

During November 1990 I was not feeling too good again and this time my waterworks were not as they should be. The doctor admitted me to Gosnells hospital and after some tests he told me that my kidneys are not too good. He did give the problem a fancy name but I forget what that was.

Upon my discharge from hospital I found that my little car had been broken into again. The locking fuel cap was gone and most of the fuel was missing too. Lance had told me to keep the tank full as it would prevent the build-up of moisture in the tank but now it was empty. I must be getting old as with the medical problems that I have been having and this break-in, I just needed a break, so Lorna picked me up and had me stay with them in their lovely home for a few days until I was feeling better.

Early in 1991, Marjory takes me on a driving holiday. It is the first trip that I have done without Lance. We drove down to Denmark where we stayed in a motel. It was such a joy to spend some time with my big sister Dorothy who is living in a retirement section of the local hospital. We took her out on a drive to visit the beach and around the town. After two nights in the motel we began our drive home. I wanted to drive through Katanning and Woodanilling where I lived as a child. It brought back a lot of memories as we drive past the old house, the old church at Marracoonda, the old school site at Mean Mahn. Then we had enough time to visit with one of my oldest friends whom I had not met up with for years. Vera Beeck was a little girl when I was born and I was told that I was named after her. Our next stop was to visit Bill and Janet Robinson who had moved down from Keysbrook to Arthur River with their family in the 1980's to take up wheat and sheep farming.

We stayed there for the night and caught up on so much information about them and their ventures. The next day Marjory returned me home again. It was such a lovely trip and brought back so many memories of my younger years. I said to Marjory when she dropped me off at home, that we must do this again sometime.

Our Christmas celebrations were a little difficult this year as this is the first time the family had been together without Lance with us. It was sad but the family lifted my spirits.

In February I was feeling off again so the doctor had me admitted for a CAT scan and a kidney biopsy. He said that it showed that my kidneys were not functioning very well and this would also cause a problem with my heart. He said something about an enzyme that the kidneys produce to make the heart work properly but that was too complicated for me to grasp. I really did not want to know what the problem was, I just wanted it to go away and leave me in peace.

When we left the farm and moved to Armadale we sold the one hundred acre hill block that we had up on Kingsbury Drive. The Buddhists bought it from us and built themselves a monastery in the bush. It always was such a peaceful little place and we were glad for them to have the use of it. But a bush fire in the area caused them to have to evacuate as the fires raged right up to the buildings.

Into February 1991 and I'm back in hospital again with the same kidney disorder. The doctor takes me off the cortisone that he had me on for a while to see if that will help. The surgeon has me in the operating theatre to carry out the carpel tunnel operation and this will help the numbness and pain that I had been suffering in my hand. I was home again in the afternoon with my hand bandaged.

In the middle of March the Amaroo Village hires a bus and a load of us take a day trip down south and spend a bit of time looking around Bunbury. It was such a lovely day with so many of the village residents who liked similar things to me. It was a very enjoyable and refreshing day.

The day after the Bunbury trip I was not feeling very well at all. After pondering everything that was going on in my life I felt that I should write out a new will. After I was satisfied of the way I had set it out, I had the lovely lady from next door witness my signature to complete the will. Lance had suggested the way it was written before but I wanted to make just a few changes.

It is the nineteenth of March 1991 and I am not feeling very well at all. There's a pain in my side and my angina is playing up again. I have difficulty in moving around. Yesterday I phoned Marjory and she was going to take me to Dangin for the weekend. She has met this nice man who has a house there and she was to going to take me for a visit. She was to finish her work in a few weeks and wanted me to see the new home she was going to move into. I was quite looking forward to that time with Marjory and Ron.

I phoned Marjory at her work and explained to her the discomfort that I was experiencing and with my breathing difficulty as well. Before I phoned her, I had one of my neighbours come and sit with me for a while and it was her suggestion that I should phone Marjory and talk to her as she would know what to do. Marjory told me to phone Lorna and the doctor as she was still working in the Pinjarra Hospital and an hour's drive away and was going to leave in a few minutes.

Lorna was at the house by the time Marjory arrived and shortly the ambulance arrived too. Apparently Lorna had ordered this to take me to hospital.

The next thing I remember is that I am in the ambulance with Marjory and the doctor on the way to Fremantle hospital as that's where they can best look after me.

I am very short of breath.

I have a pain in my chest and my side aches.

A face mask covers my mouth and nose and I can hear the oxygen running into my chest and this does help me some.

I have some visions that send me back into my past. I can see Mother standing beside Father in front of the house at Mean Mahn. My sisters and brothers are there too. Dorothy is wearing the dress that she hand-made and wore to her wedding. Florrie with her cook's hat on that she wore when she used to work in the hospital kitchen in Katanning. Ray is riding the horse that we used to ride to school. Don is swinging the axe as he chops up some firewood so Mother can cook our meals. Chrissie is sitting on the ground just outside the chook-yard playing with the doll which Dorothy had made for me. The twins Molly and Myrtle are running around chasing the chook that got out of the yard. Connie is sitting on Mother's chair on the back verandah doing some needlepoint work. Margaret is sitting next to her looking on.

Pop and Mummy Gomm with me sitting beside them are in his Chev van as we drive along the road from Katanning to Armadale. The back of the van is packed with our belongings.

Lance is driving the Austin Seven as we head down to Albany for our summer holidays. The children are in the back seat. Gwen sits up so proudly while nursing little Neil on her lap. Marjory and Lorna are playing eye-spy while David is looking out the window, counting the sheep in the paddock.

I see that I am sitting at the kitchen table with Lance and the children as we read the Bible that we have done every day of my life. Then the children have grown up and left home to lead their own lives and Lance and I read the Bible with just the two of us at the table

Lance and I are with the tour group in Noumea and are heading back to the ship that will take us to our next destination.

Presently, back to reality again, I am in the hospital bed with doctors and nurses around me and everything begins to go dark.

I can feel myself slipping away from this life on earth that God has planned for me.

Perhaps when I go to heaven I can meet up with Lance again and enjoy the everlasting life that I am looking forward to.

Darkness falls upon me and I can hear the sounds around me but they too become dim as I quietly slip away from my life in the flesh on earth and begin my journey into the next life in heaven.

Photos of Importance to us

Walter Dudley Lavis, Father and Alice Emily Lavis, Mother

Mother and us in 1921 | Family at Mean Mahn 1922

Our Family in late 1923.

Twynesdale home 1923

Don and sisters 1924

Dorothy and Abel's wedding 1928. That's me on the right.

At Badgebup 1933

Me in the fashion of the day 1933

Me at 21 years of age

Lance at 21 years of age

Pop and Mummy Gomm

Our Wedding 1937

Pop with his Chev van

The "Wee Hoose" that Pop built

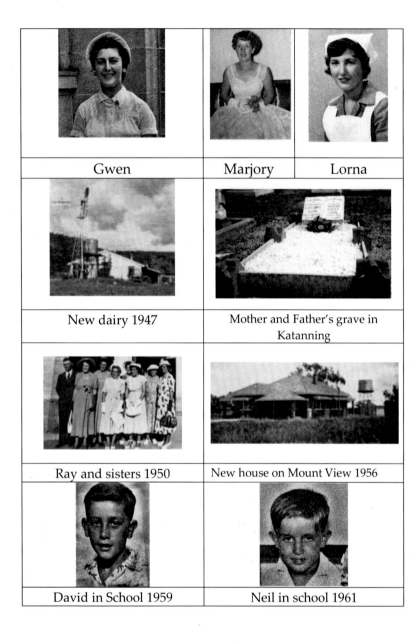

Gwen	Marjory	Lorna
New dairy 1947	Mother and Father's grave in Katanning	
Ray and sisters 1950	New house on Mount View 1956	
David in School 1959	Neil in school 1961	

Gwen and Fred's wedding 1957	Marjory and Greg's wedding 1963
Lance and I 1963	Lorna and Barry's wedding 1963
David and Barbara's wedding 1968	Lance and me again.
Janalli Way home, Armadale	Neil and Jacky's wedding 1980

249

Our new bikes	Family at Golden Wedding Anniversary

Lance and I at Golden Wedding 1987	By my parents graveside 1990

My great Grandson Riley and me. 1990

About the Author

David Kentish spent his early years on the family dairy farm just south of Perth in Western Australia near the small settlement of Keysbrook.

Before the time of broadcast television, his father, J. Lance Kentish, spent time in the evenings inventing and telling stories about the bush animals, the talking red-gum tree and the magic carpet to his family.

David has continued in this same vein with the telling of stories of imaginary Australian bush animals and friends and the many predicaments that they find themselves involved in.

David, with his wife Barbara, enjoys travelling with their 4x4 and caravan in and around the Australian outback and bush. This is where he gets most of his inspiration which has led to a collection of stories of their travels.

A Place Called Earth was written whilst on one of these trips and is an exciting collection of stories from David's point of view of how earth began and developed over many countless years. A well written yarn that will keep you intrigued right up to the last page.

David has several more stories in the pipeline so keep a look out for more stories by David Kentish.

Other books by David

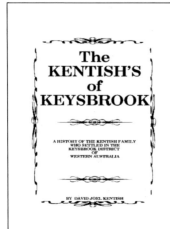

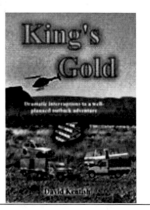

Visit his website for more detail
www.davidkentish.com.au